Also by Drew Thomas Allen

*America's Last Stand: Will You Vote to Save
or Destroy America in 2024?*

For Christ and Country: The Martyrdom of Charlie Kirk

CLINTON HOAX, OBAMA COUP

THE DECLASSIFIED STORY OF THE TRUMP-RUSSIA DELUSION

DREW THOMAS ALLEN

Published by Bombardier Books
An Imprint of Post Hill Press
ISBN: 979-8-89565-543-6
ISBN (eBook): 979-8-89565-544-3

Clinton Hoax, Obama Coup:
The Declassified Story of the Trump–Russia Delusion
© 2026 by Drew Thomas Allen
All Rights Reserved

Cover Design by Conroy Accord
Cover Photo by Gage Skidmore

This book, as well as any other Bombardier Books publications, may be purchased in bulk quantities at a special discounted rate. Contact orders@bombardierbooks.com for more information.

Post Hill Press
New York • Nashville
posthillpress.com

Published in the United States of America
1 2 3 4 5 6 7 8 9 10

TABLE OF CONTENTS

INTRODUCTION

t has been a decade since the American people were subjected to one of the most destructive political hoaxes in modern history, possibly in all American history: the Trump–Russia collusion narrative.

Sold to the public as fact, it was in truth a complete fabrication, premediated, highly orchestrated, and launched by Hillary Clinton's allies. It was then amplified by partisan operatives embedded in the intelligence community, the media, and the Democratic Party.

Many of the existing books on the Russia hoax—such as Lee Smith's *The Plot Against the President* (2019), Gregg Jarrett's *The Russia Hoax* (2018), Andrew McCarthy's *Ball of Collusion* (2019), and Byron York's *Obsession* (2020), to name a few—have established a consistent foundation of facts: that the Trump–Russia collusion narrative originated with the Clinton campaign's opposition research (the Steele dossier); that senior officials in the FBI, DOJ, and intelligence community knowingly used dubious evidence to justify surveillance of Trump's campaign; and that the media acted as an echo chamber to legitimize the false story.

Those authors could smell a rat long before official investigations caught up. They were persuasive, fact-driven, and grounded in what information was available. But ultimately, they were limited by inability to access classified material buried by the very bureaucrats who had orchestrated the hoax.

Subsequent investigations, such as Inspector General Michael Horowitz's 2019 report and Special Counsel John Durham's 2023 findings, confirmed that the FBI relied on flimsy evidence, political bias, and unverified opposition research in pursuing the Trump–Russia collusion narrative. Most of these findings came only after a wave of books had already been published. In that sense, these authors were vindicated. But the investigations also buried the full extent of the corruption by classifying and withholding critical evidence.

Long before I was an author and publicist, I was a college student in Florence, Italy, where I fell in love with the Renaissance. I've spent countless hours wandering museums across Europe, especially in Rome and Florence.

A few years ago, I returned to the Uffizi in Florence with my wife, our six-month-old daughter strapped to my chest, and my mother-in-law in tow. Navigating the crowded galleries with nap schedules and the occasional waft from a poopy diaper was a far cry from the carefree visits of my youth. I was headed for the exit—gelato and a Negroni were calling my name—when a special exhibit stopped me cold.

I was awestruck by an enormous painting on the wall. Only it wasn't quite a painting. Leonardo Da Vinci's *Adoration of the Magi* shows the Virgin Mary with the infant Jesus surrounded by the Magi, but it remains at the underpainting stage—the monochrome first layer mapping light, shadow, and composition before color is added. After a six-year restoration cleared away centuries of yellowed varnish, grime, and even later overpainting, hidden details emerged: swirling crowds, rearing horses, and crumbling ruins, all in sharp relief.

In its unfinished state, the work offers a rare, unobstructed view of Leonardo's original brushstrokes and creative process—details that would have vanished beneath layers of paint. It was the blueprint for a masterpiece that never reached completion, preserving the raw architecture of his vision in a way no finished painting ever could.

Just as Leonardo's *Adoration of the Magi* lay hidden beneath centuries of varnish and overpainting, so too was the truth about the Trump–Russia collusion narrative obscured under layers of distortion. The complexity and breadth of the operation were disguised by a tangled web of agencies, actors, and acronyms that made it nearly impossible for the average American to follow. New fabrications and lies were layered on top of the old, each designed to cover the cracks as previous claims collapsed. A media eager to apply its own coatings manipulated and changed the image with endless propaganda, selective leaks, and breathless headlines. All this was intended to hide the reality beneath.

Even the Horowitz and Durham investigations failed to restore the true image. Both reports confirmed the surface flaws—flimsy evidence, political bias, reliance on opposition research—but left the most damning details buried under layers of classification. What emerged was only a partial restoration, enough to vindicate those who had long suspected foul play but not enough to reveal the full extent of the crime.

Had Donald Trump not been reelected in 2024, the truth would have remained buried, condemned to rot beneath layers of varnish and deception, its outlines fading further with each passing year.

Thanks to Tulsi Gabbard, Trump's Director of National Intelligence, a full restoration of the scheme is underway. Her declassification of the documents that Horowitz and Durham buried has stripped away the final layers of varnish and over-painting, allowing the original blueprint to emerge in full. And boy, is it ugly.

A critical March 31, 2016 meeting marks one of the earliest signposts in the life of the hoax. On that day, senior FBI leadership—including Deputy Director Andrew McCabe—met with top DOJ officials to discuss fresh intelligence reports from the CIA. Those reports indicated that Hillary Clinton's campaign was developing a plan to link Donald Trump to Russia to deflect attention from her own email scandal, and worse, as I will later explain. This was months before Crossfire Hurricane, the FBI's investigation into alleged Trump–Russia ties, was officially launched. The very officials who would later greenlight surveillance of the Trump campaign already knew that the "Russia narrative" traced back to Clinton's political strategy. Even as they dismissed the "raw intelligence" warning of Clinton's plan, those same FBI and DOJ officials moved forward with building a case against Trump based on similar "raw intelligence."

So too did those same FBI and DOJ officials possess intelligence suggesting a backchannel between Attorney General Loretta Lynch and the Clinton campaign. That reporting indicated that Lynch was keeping Clinton's team informed about the progress of the email investigation. Instead of treating this as evidence of a compromised Justice Department, officials buried it alongside the Clinton plan intelligence. The nation's top law enforcement agency was tilting its scales, ignoring conflicts of interest at the very top, and shielding Clinton while simultaneously moving against Trump.

We have also learned that President Obama personally ordered the Intelligence Community Assessment (ICA) on Russian interference in the 2016 election. That directive, issued in December 2016 after Trump had already won, ensured that the outgoing administration could sabotage and undermine the incoming Trump presidency. What should have been a dead hoax was suddenly revived, elevated with the weight of an "official" intelligence product, and weaponized against the incoming president.

The ICA gave the collusion narrative a veneer of legitimacy, transforming it from campaign dirty trick into government-certified "truth." In doing so, Obama's order breathed new life into the operation and advanced it into something far more dangerous: not just a hoax, but the opening salvo of a coup against a duly elected president. In short, the Clinton Hoax became an Obama coup.

This book finally puts the pieces together. Now, with the full restoration nearing completion, the picture is plain to see—and it is far darker than anyone could have believed.

The collusion operation required the participation of a sitting president, a presidential nominee, the directors of the FBI and CIA, the Director of National Intelligence, a partisan law firm (Perkins Coie), an opposition research firm (Fusion GPS), and a complicit media machine that worked not as watchdogs, but as propagandists. This attempted heist of our nation makes *Ocean's Eleven* look like amateur hour.

And while the operation was complex by design, my goal is to explain it so clearly that even a kindergartner can understand it. And kindergartners *should* understand it—because it's the greatest threat to the American republic since the Civil War. Not in the past, but at present. The threat is still active.

This is not a dry retelling of a political scandal. America has not recovered or moved on. Nor can we until every American knows the truth and those involved are held accountable.

The poison of 2016 continues to course through our nation and our institutions. The rot began with Benghazi in 2012, metastasized in 2016, escalated in 2020, and nearly destroyed the country in the lead-up to 2024. But the focus of this book is on the series of events that took place immediately after September 11, 2012, which culminated in Trump–Russia collusion. The infection that started with Benghazi in 2012 spread nationwide four years later.

And make no mistake: Crimes were committed. That's not hyperbole or a conspiracy theory. That's reality.

Kevin Clinesmith, an FBI lawyer, pleaded guilty in 2020 to altering an email to justify renewing a Foreign Intelligence Surveillance Act (FISA) warrant to spy on Carter Page, an American citizen and Trump campaign advisor.

Someone illegally leaked the classified content of a phone call between General Michael Flynn and Russian Ambassador Sergey Kislyak. That was a felony. To this day, we don't know who did it. The leaker is still out there.

Andrew McCabe, former FBI Deputy Director, lied at least four times—three under oath—to federal investigators about authorizing leaks related to the Clinton Foundation probe. No consequences.

James Comey, McCabe's boss and then FBI Director, leaked classified memos of his conversations with President Trump, giving them to a friend to feed to the press, deliberately triggering the Mueller investigation. He was indicted by a Grand Jury on charges of lying to Congress and obstruction of Justice in late

September 2025, a stunning reversal for the man once lionized by the press as a defender of democracy.

But in November 2025, a Clinton-appointed federal judge abruptly threw out the case—not because Comey was proven innocent, but on a procedural technicality. The court ruled that the acting U.S. Attorney who secured the indictment had been improperly appointed, rendering the entire prosecution an "unlawful exercise of executive power." In other words, the charges evaporated not on the facts, but on a paperwork dispute.

It was a sharp reminder of the double standard that has defined this era. In a system that has bent over backward to shield Democratic elites, there is still no guarantee Comey will ever face the same consequences that Trump allies have endured for far less.

John Brennan, CIA Director, testified under oath that the Steele dossier wasn't used in the Intelligence Community Assessment on Russian interference. Evidence shows it was, indicating that Brennan lied to Congress.

Are you getting the point?

Years may have passed since you last gazed upon the galleries filled with snapshots of the Russia hoax—headlines, hearings, dossiers, and denials, each one framed and hung as if it revealed the truth. But now I invite you to return with fresh eyes. Grab a Negroni or a gelato and settle in, because I am going to take you to the special exhibit—one curated not by spin doctors or partisan reporters, but unveiled through the declassifications of Tulsi Gabbard, Trump's Director of National Intelligence.

At last, the curtain has been pulled back, the varnish stripped away, and the raw underpainting revealed. What it shows is no masterpiece. This is the blueprint of a hoax turned coup.

And it all started with Benghazi.

CHAPTER ONE

AMERICA'S FIRST MUSLIM PRESIDENT

A major pillar of Obama's reelection effort was his alleged success against al-Qaeda. He had greenlit the raid that killed Osama bin Laden and ran ads declaring, "Bin Laden is dead. al-Qaeda is on the run." The message was clear: Thanks to Obama, terrorism was in retreat.

In his September 8, 2012 weekly address—just days before the eleventh anniversary of 9/11—Obama beamed with pride as he declared, "We took the fight to al Qaeda, decimated their leadership, and put them on a path to defeat.… Osama bin Laden will never threaten America again."[1]

But Obama's self-congratulatory celebration was premature; worse, it was dangerously divorced from reality. It was true that Bin Laden—al-Qaeda's leader and the mastermind of the deadliest terrorist attacks in US history—was dead. But it was delusional to suggest that the threat of global terrorism was in retreat.

Al-Qaeda affiliates were rapidly expanding in strength, resources, and territory. These groups were gaining influence, control, and new footholds in regions that previously had no significant terrorist presence. One of those new regions that had been overrun by radical Islamist terrorist groups was the country of Libya.

The Obama administration spearheaded the NATO-led intervention to overthrow Libyan strongman Muammar Gaddafi in 2011, providing critical airpower, logistical support, and the facilitation of arms to rebel forces—many of whom were radical Islamist fighters—to topple Gaddafi.

Muammar Gaddafi—a brutal but secular dictator—was killed, and the power vacuum this created was quickly filled by warring militias and radical Islamist factions, including al-Qaeda affiliates. These affiliates operated independently of al-Qaeda but were committed to the same core mission: waging global jihad, overthrowing secular governments like Libya, and imposing Sharia law in its place.

Sharia law is the legal code that terrorists like al-Qaeda, ISIS, and the Taliban enforce to justify murder, slavery, and oppression. Thieves have their hands cut off, adulterers are stoned to death, children are forced into marriage, women are flogged or veiled into silence, and "infidels" are slaughtered in the name of jihad.

After Gaddafi's fall, Libya's unguarded weapons arsenals were ransacked by everyone from militias to civilians, turning the country into a jihadist arms bazaar, with Gaddafi's stockpiles flooding into the hands of terrorists across North Africa and the Middle East.

Obama's foreign policy, especially as it related to the Middle East, was objectively a disaster. He hadn't defeated the terrorists.

Instead, he had helped facilitate the circumstances under which they could rapidly expand in both numbers and strength.

It was disingenuous at best when Obama campaigned on and took credit for the weakening of al-Qaeda and a dead Bin Laden—not because it was untrue that al-Qaeda had been weakened or that Bin Laden had been killed under the Obama administration, but because the United States had been at war with al-Qaeda for almost eleven years on September 8, 2012.

Bin Laden narrowly escaped capture by Delta Force operators at Tora Bora in December 2001. So, while Bin Laden's death represented the culmination of a concerted effort that spanned two administrations and nearly a decade of relentless pursuit, those who hailed this as the end failed to recognize the present reality.

Al-Qaeda may have been "on the run," but Obama's disastrous foreign policy—especially in Libya—created the perfect conditions for dozens of new jihadist groups and al-Qaeda affiliates to rise in its place. He had cut off the head of the hydra only to unleash a swarm of new heads and even new hydras, each more vicious than the last.

Obama had always been unusually and reflexively defensive of the Islamic religion. During the same September 8, 2012 weekly address, after praising his administration for putting "al Qaeda on a path to defeat" and killing Osama bin Laden, he made sure to follow "Obama's Golden rule": Never mention Islamic terrorists without also defending Islam.[2]

"I have always said that America is at war with al Qaeda and its affiliates," he said, "and we will never be at war with Islam or any other religion."

The issue wasn't so much that Obama was sympathetic towards the religion of Islam, even if he seemed to regard it with a favoritism he didn't extend to any other faith. The issue was that his affection for the religion was so overpowering, it blinded him to the ideological motivations of the Islamic terrorists.

It is irrelevant that there are more peaceful Muslims than radical jihadists. As a comparison, there are more than two hundred dog breeds. One study concluded that over a thirteen-year period between January 2005 and December 2017, 433 Americans were killed by dogs. Pit bulls were responsible for 66 percent of those deaths.[3]

A special interest group of pit bull breeders or owners with a deep personal and emotionally driven interest in defending the breed might say the actions of a few violent pitbulls do not represent the many pit bulls that haven't killed people. Obviously, not every pit bull is a killer. But the reality is that not every pit bull has to maul, maim, or kill for it to be true that this breed is disproportionately dangerous compared to others. Why aren't golden retrievers, labradoodles, French bulldogs, or King Charles spaniels making the headlines for deadly attacks? A rational observer can see that something about the pit bull breed—whether rooted in breeding, temperament, or instinct—makes it uniquely predisposed to violence. Recognizing this fact doesn't mean condemning every pit bull, especially those that have never attacked anyone. But if your worldview insists that all pit bulls are docile and nonviolent, then each attack is an inconvenient contradiction to your narrative.

Obama's thesis on Islam wasn't that there were only "a few" violent Muslims carrying out terrorist attacks. It was that Islamic terrorism had *nothing* to do with Islam at all—a complete dissociation that ignored the ideological motivations the terrorists themselves openly claimed. Worse, Obama tried to create a false moral equivalence that other religions were equally prone to this kind of violence. But there is simply no modern comparison. No other major religion today produces a sustained, organized, transnational pattern of ideological violence on this scale.

For example, Obama stood behind a podium in a room filled with American Christians at the National Prayer Breakfast in February 2015 and lectured, "During the Crusades and the Inquisition, people committed terrible deeds in the name of Christ. In our home country, slavery and Jim Crow were often justified in the name of Christ."[4]

The Crusades ended more than seven hundred years ago. Slavery in America was abolished over one hundred fifty years ago, and Jim Crow ended half a century ago. The Crusades themselves were largely territorial wars between Muslims and Christians over Jerusalem, not remotely comparable to jihadists waging a global holy war in the present day. Slavery and Jim Crow (both championed by Democrats) were not carried out in the name of Christianity or any other religion. Today, there are zero Christian theocracies, zero global Christian recruitment networks for holy war, zero Christian governments executing apostates, and zero Christian movements seeking to impose a worldwide dictatorship under a "successor of Jesus Christ," as Islam aims to do with a Caliphate.

On February 3, 2016—almost exactly one year after lecturing Christians at the National Prayer Breakfast and drawing a false moral equivalence between Christians and jihadists—Obama spoke at the Islamic Society of Baltimore. "This mosque," he declared, "like so many in our country, is an all-American story." What was he talking about? Mosques aren't an all-American story. The pilgrims who fled religious persecution and landed at Plymouth Rock weren't Muslims—they were English Protestants. And the document they signed upon arrival, the Mayflower

Compact, made their purpose unmistakably clear: they undertook the voyage *"for the glory of God and the advancement of the Christian faith."* America's foundations were laid by Christians, built upon Christian conviction, and rooted in a distinctly Christian moral order—not imams and Islamic institutions.[5]

The Founding Fathers who enshrined religious liberty in the Constitution weren't Muslims, nor did they worship in mosques. America's religious heritage, from the colonies through the Revolution, was overwhelmingly Christian, rooted in the Judeo-Christian values that shaped our laws, culture, and moral framework. To portray mosques as part of that heritage wasn't inclusivity—it was historical revisionism.

"You've been part of this city for nearly half a century," Obama said. Yet the Pilgrims landed at Plymouth Rock in 1620, and the Declaration of Independence was signed in 1776. A mosque in Baltimore built less than fifty years ago is an "all-American story"? Why? Because the same American Christians Obama so often accused of Islamophobia after Islamic terrorist attacks actually upheld religious liberty, protecting Muslims' right to worship instead of burning down mosques or attacking them in the streets?[6]

Obama would then go on to lecture the room of Muslims about how they had racism in their DNA because of the Arab Muslim slave trade—which for over a thousand years transported millions of Africans across the Middle East and North Africa. He would remind them that this slave trade predated the transatlantic slave trade by centuries, lasted far longer, and was fueled by Islamic empires and merchants who captured, castrated, and sold African (and European) men, women, and children to buyers from India, China, North Africa, and the Ottoman Empire.

I'm kidding, of course. He never gave that speech, because Obama's "moral equivalence" sermons were reserved for Christians, never Muslims. Obama was the Billy Graham of Islam in America—the most powerful and influential champion of the religion in the nation's history.

Obama spent the rest of his speech at the Islamic Society of Baltimore lavishing praise on the Muslim audience—telling them how wonderful they were, how grateful he was for their contributions, and, of course, apologizing on behalf of America for the way those "nasty" Christians supposedly blamed them for "the violent acts of the few."

While Obama reflexively defended the institution of Islam and dismissed acts of terrorism as "the violent acts of the few," he also attacked other institutions such as law enforcement, portraying deadly encounters between Blacks and police as evidence of "a systematic problem."

A single day of Islamic terrorism on 9/11 killed more Americans than ten years' worth of police shootings of Black men combined. Yet Obama never concluded that was evidence of "a systematic problem" with Muslims or Islam. Nor did he reach that conclusion after repeated Islamist terror acts during his presidency.[7]

Obama's love of Islam might have been rooted in his idolization of his Kenyan, Muslim father, who abandoned him. Or it might have stemmed from the four years he spent immersed in Muslim culture in Jakarta, Indonesia, with his mother and her new Muslim, Indonesian husband, Barry Soetoro. I don't know. Probably both experiences shaped his beliefs. What I do know is that Obama never took the threat of terrorism seriously. He couldn't because his worldview prevented it. Islamic terrorism and Islam were not the same.

Obama's narrative about Islam—and one I think he sincerely believed—was that Islam is a peaceful religion to be revered. In the same way that Obama idolized the father he never knew, creating a flawless, heroic image in his mind that ignored inconvenient facts, he similarly romanticized Islam.

The United States suffered a wave of deadly Islamist-inspired attacks during the Obama Administration. Each one contradicted and threatened to shatter Obama's delusional worldview. But he was more invested in shielding Islam from criticism and maintaining his fictionalized narrative than he was in preventing Americans from being killed by Islamic terrorists.

The upshot of this was a built-in conflict of interest that warped his approach to national security. Externally, Obama understood that the American public expected the president of the United States to address the increasing number of terrorist attacks within the country. Internally, he felt that doing so would damage the image of a religion he felt compelled to protect.

Obama was America's first Muslim president not because he was a Muslim (as he claimed to be a Christian), but because he governed as if defending the image of Islam was a central obligation of his presidency. The lengths he was willing to go in pursuit of this mission would alter the course of American history. He politicized the intelligence agencies, weaponized the Pentagon, and corrupted the machinery of government to shield Islam and prop up his own delusional worldview. In fact, before the Benghazi hoax and the Trump–Russia collusion hoax, there was another hoax: Obama's "workplace violence" hoax.

On November 5, 2009, licensed psychiatrist and US Army major Nidal Hasan entered the Soldier Readiness Center at Fort Hood in Killeen, Texas, armed with two pistols. He jumped up on a desk, shouted "Allahu Akbar!" ("God is great!"), and opened fire. Twelve soldiers and one Department of Defense employee were murdered. Thirty-two others were wounded.[8]

When President Obama addressed the attack that evening at the Tribal Nations Conference at the Department of the Interior, it had been two and a half hours since the mass shooting had taken place around 2:30 p.m. eastern time. News of the attack had already been widely reported by the media.

Reading from prepared remarks, Obama told the audience, "We will make sure that we get answers to every single question about this horrible incident."[9]

Even as reports emerged in the following weeks confirming that the attack was an act of Islamic terrorism, Obama couldn't quite bring himself to admit it. "We cannot fully know what leads a man to do such a thing," Obama said during his weekly address on November 7, 2009. Nevertheless, he remained fully committed to solving the mystery that wasn't. He added reassuringly: "On Friday I met with FBI Director Robert Mueller, Defense Secretary Gates, and representatives of the relevant agencies to discuss their ongoing investigation into what led to this terrible crime."[10]

Crime? It was terrorist attack, and he knew it. They all knew it.

Five days after the attack, on November 9, 2009, *The New York Times* published an article with the headline: "U.S. Knew of Suspect's Tie to Radical Cleric." The *Times* reported that intelligence agencies had intercepted as many as twenty emails sent between Army Major Nidal Hasan and Anwar al-Awlaki before the attack, dating all the way back to December of 2008—nearly a year before the shooting.[11]

Anwar al-Awlaki, the US-born son of Yemeni parents, went from preaching in American mosques to becoming one of al-Qaeda's most dangerous assets. While posing as a "moderate" imam in San Diego and later at the Dar al-Hijrah mosque in Virginia, he cultivated ties to at least three of the 9/11 hijackers and quietly embraced jihadist ideology.

In March 2002, with the FBI circling and possible criminal charges looming due to passport fraud, he slipped out of the country to Yemen, where he quickly deepened his involvement with al-Qaeda in the Arabian Peninsula. Over the next few years, he emerged as one of al-Qaeda's top recruiters and English-language propagandists. His sermons and writings, especially in the terrorist-run *Inspire* magazine, didn't just preach hate. They motivated Army Major Nidal Hasan—and others—to carry out terrorist attacks.[12]

Hasan reached out to the al-Qaeda leader. In messages, Hasan asked Awlaki if it was permissible for a Muslim soldier to kill US soldiers if they are fighting Muslims and suggested that "suicide bombing is permissible in certain cases."[13]

Hasan forwarded anti-US surveys, offered to donate to al-Awlaki's website, writing to al-Awlaki in an email—"Please have alternative to donate…assure privacy for some who are concerned,"—and even promoted a "$5,000.00 scholarship prize…entitled 'Why is Anwar Al Awlaki a great activist and leader.'"[14]

Al-Awlaki's replies validated Hasan's grievances without explicitly ordering violence. The FBI reviewed the exchanges but deemed them harmless "research" months before Hasan murdered thirteen people.

On the same day that Hasan carried out the attack, al-Awlaki praised the shooting in a post on his English language website: "Nidal Hasan is a hero. He is a man of conscience who could not bear living the contradiction of being a Muslim and serving in an army that is fighting against his own people."[15]

Was there any doubt about what motivated the Ford Hood shooting?

The New York Times reported on November 14, 2009, that in the days after the Fort Hood massacre, investigators searching Major Nidal Hasan's apartment near the base discovered a box of his personal effects. Inside were business cards he had printed for himself. Alongside his name and Army rank, the cards bore the chilling self-designation "SoA"—shorthand for "Soldier of Allah." Hasan had openly branded himself as a jihadist long before he opened fire.[16]

A Muslim army major with business cards proclaiming himself a Soldier of Allah, who had been corresponding with a known al-Qaeda leader for the past year, entered a facility at a US Army post in central Texas, jumped onto a table shouting "Allahu Akbar," and opened fire with two handguns, killing thirteen Americans. With the possible exception of the business cards that overtly described his new occupation as an Islamist terrorist, all of this was known to the FBI and President Obama immediately after the attack. Obama certainly knew before *The New York Times* reported it on November 9. By the time he delivered his Weekly Address on November 14, he already had all the evidence he needed to determine Hasan's motives, worldview, and contacts. But he didn't.

"There is an ongoing investigation into this terrible tragedy," Obama said instead. "That investigation will look at the motives of the alleged gunman, including his views and contacts." These mysterious "views" were spelled out for all to see on his business cards.

Nidal Hasan had given a class presentation in the spring of 2007 while serving as a psychiatry resident at the Uniformed Services University of the Health Sciences (USUHS) in Bethesda,

Maryland. According to multiple sources, including the Senate Homeland Security's 2011 report *A Ticking Time Bomb*, Hasan used the opportunity not to present on a medical subject, but to justify violent jihad, going so far as to explain when killing civilians could be acceptable under Islamic law. Classmates and even an officer in the room reported his remarks to superiors, but instead of disciplinary action, the incident was quietly buried in an informal evaluation. This was two full years before the FBI began intercepting his emails with Anwar al-Awlaki, the al-Qaeda cleric.

Obama admitted that, on the evening of the attack, he met in the Oval Office with Secretary of Defense Robert Gates, Chairman of the Joint Chiefs Admiral Mike Mullen, and FBI Director Robert Mueller—and then again the next morning with senior military and intelligence officials. Publicly, Obama claimed to be searching for motives. Privately, he was orchestrating the rebranding of an act of Islamic terrorism into mere "workplace violence."

The workplace violence hoax was already hiding in plain sight.

Obama ordered his cabinet and FBI Director Robert Mueller "to review the immediate steps that were necessary to support the families and secure Fort Hood."[17] He also ordered the leadership of the military and intelligence community "to undertake a full review of the sequence of events that led up to the shootings."[18]

The Pentagon's review was finished in January 2010. Titled "Protecting the Force: Lessons from Fort Hood," the Department of Defense review managed to examine every aspect of the Fort Hood massacre except the one that was relevant—its nature as an act of jihadist terrorism from within the US Army. Instead, the report sanitized the attack as "workplace violence."[19]

By refusing to identify Major Nidal Hasan's radical Islamist motivation or to classify his rampage as terrorism, the Department of Defense avoided confronting the reality of internal extremist threats. The choice wasn't just semantics; it downplayed the role of jihadist ideology and denied the victims and their families the recognition and benefits afforded to combat casualties of terrorism. Perhaps most telling: Major Nidal Hassan wasn't mentioned by name a single time in the Pentagon's review.[20]

Barely a month after the attack, in December 2009, FBI Director Robert Mueller quietly commissioned an "independent review" of the Bureau's handling of Nidal Hasan before the attack was carried out.[21] Former FBI and CIA chief William H. Webster's final report wasn't released until July 19, 2012, more than two and a half years later.

That report included Hasan's communications with al-Qaeda cleric Anwar al-Awlaki but made no effort to conclude that the attack was an act of jihadist terrorism. That's because the Webster Commission was purposely not tasked with determining Hasan's motives, views, or contacts; its sole mandate was to scrutinize the FBI's own actions, identify potential mistakes, and recommend policy changes. In other words, because the commission's mission excluded any examination of motive, it ensured that the Obama administration's decision to disregard the obvious terrorism element while falsely defining the slaughter as "workplace violence" would remain unchallenged.

Obama had been president for less than ten months at the time of the Fort Hood shooting, which wasn't even the first jihadist attack under his administration. That had occurred on June 1, 2009, when Abdulhakim Mujahid Muhammad—a Muslim convert formerly known as Carlos Bledsoe—opened fire on an Army recruiting station in Little Rock, Arkansas.[22]

Private William Long was killed, and Private Quinton Ezeagwula was wounded. Muhammad was arrested shortly after the attack and told investigators it was an "act of war" against the US military.[23] He cited his time in Yemen and claimed ties to al-Qaeda in the Arabian Peninsula as his motivation.

Carlos Bledsoe, born in Memphis, Tennessee, converted to Islam in 2004 and later adopted his new name, Abdulhakim Mujahid Muhammad. In 2007, he traveled to Yemen, where he studied Arabic and Islam, married a Yemeni woman, and came into contact with individuals connected to al-Qaeda in the Arabian Peninsula. Yemeni authorities arrested him in 2008 for immigration violations and suspected militant ties before deporting him to the United States in early 2009. Within months of his return, Muhammad carried out the Little Rock recruiting station shooting.[24]

In a statement released by the White House, Obama said he was "deeply saddened by this senseless violence."[25] But it was not senseless. The Muslim convert and terrorist had already told police that he had "political and religious" motives, which was recorded in court records.

Despite Abdulhakim Mujahid Muhammad's admission, the attack was not prosecuted as a federal terrorism case. Federal prosecutors deferred to Arkansas authorities, who pursued state charges of capital murder and attempted murder.

The Obama administration maintained that the evidence did not establish a direct operational link between Muhammad and a foreign terrorist organization sufficient to sustain a terrorism charge in court. As a result, the attack was handled entirely in state court and was never officially designated a federal terrorism case.[26]

Why, then, did the Obama administration adopt the opposite approach when it came to Dylann Roof?

Dylann Roof was a white supremacist who murdered nine African American parishioners at Emanuel AME Church in Charleston, South Carolina, on June 17, 2015. Although South Carolina had already charged Roof with multiple counts of capital murder and could seek the death penalty, federal prosecutors pursued hate crime charges and obstruction of religious exercise resulting in death, both of which also carried the death penalty.[27]

The case proceeded in federal court, resulting in Roof's conviction and death sentence in 2016. The decision to bring federal charges despite overlapping state jurisdiction demonstrated that, when the administration saw political or symbolic value, it was willing to take full federal control of a murder case—something it had declined to do in the Little Rock attack, even though the perpetrator openly admitted to being inspired by al-Qaeda in the Arabian Peninsula.

I think it's obvious why the Obama administration declined to prosecute Abdulhakim Mujahid Muhammad in federal court. A federal terrorism trial would have required the government to present, in open court, the evidence that Muhammad's actions were inspired by al-Qaeda in the Arabian Peninsula. That, in turn, would have meant officially acknowledging that the first successful terrorist attack on US soil during Obama's presidency was an act of Islamist terrorism—just months before the even deadlier Fort Hood massacre and a few years before Benghazi. By keeping the case in Arkansas state court, the administration avoided the public and political fallout that would have come with admitting that jihadist violence was not just a distant, foreign threat, but a growing danger inside the United States.

There was a new sheriff in town, and his name was Barack Hussein Obama. In just the first year of his presidency, America suffered three jihadist-motivated attacks or attempts: the June 2009 Little Rock recruiting station shooting, the November 2009 Fort Hood massacre, and the Christmas Day "underwear bomber" plot—which failed only because the device malfunctioned, and alert passengers and crew subdued the attacker. But America's first Muslim, half-white president was only getting started. His refusal to recognize the Little Rock shooting as terrorism, coupled with his politicization of the intelligence agencies to steer investigations away from politically inconvenient truths and toward his own delusional, self-serving narratives, was merely the appetizer in Obama's full banquet of corruption.

Obama had already proven he was willing to lie, distort the truth, and weaponize government to protect himself and his agenda. Few could have imagined just how far he was willing to go. That revelation came three years later when the Benghazi attack exposed the full measure of his duplicity—and the extraordinary lengths to which his administration would go to bury the truth. Americans had elected a monster. And he was only getting started.

CHAPTER TWO

OBAMA AND THE TERRIBLE, HORRIBLE, NO GOOD, VERY BAD DAY

t was a warm, dry night in Benghazi on September 11. Inside the walled garden of the Temporary Mission Facility, palm fronds swayed gently under a moonlit sky. US Ambassador J. Christopher Stevens and Information Management Officer Sean Smith had retired to the main residence for the evening. Smith, just thirty-four years old, was an Air Force veteran, a devoted husband, and a father of two. His wife, Heather, and their young children remained in The Hague, awaiting his return once this temporary posting in Benghazi came to an end.[28]

Ambassador Stevens had only just arrived from Tripoli the day before. What he found was alarming. Law and order had collapsed, local police could not be trusted, and radical Islamist militias roamed the streets unchecked. al-Qaeda–linked groups like Ansar al-Sharia were growing bolder, threatening US and Western interests, and Stevens had already received reports of suspicious surveillance of the compound.[29]

Ambassador Stevens had communicated all these warnings to the State Department earlier that very day. Yet only five US agents were on duty that night—two traveling with Stevens and three permanently stationed in Benghazi.[30] It was a skeleton crew. All summer, Stevens had sent formal requests for more security, more agents, and more resources. The State Department, under Secretary of State Hillary Clinton, had repeatedly declined.

In the months before the Benghazi attack, Ambassador Stevens had warned Washington of escalating dangers. Cables dated July 25 and August 2 warned that security was "unpredictable and deteriorating," and that Libya remained "volatile and violent."[31] Stevens's August 15 emergency meeting with the Regional Security Officer concluded the compound was indefensible against a "coordinated attack."[32] Stevens cabled Washington these warnings the next day. And on the morning of September 11, Stevens sent a three-page cable detailing dire risks due to local militias threatening to withdraw support, Libyan forces incapable of providing even basic protection, and extremist groups steadily gaining strength.[33]

Ambassador Stevens and his team understood the symbolism of the date, which was solemn enough for Americans, but potentially deadly in Libya. That morning, Sean Smith messaged a friend with grim foreboding: "Assuming we don't die tonight... we saw one of our 'police' taking pictures."

At about 9:40 p.m., gunfire erupted outside the US Special Mission compound in Benghazi. Attackers quickly breached the perimeter. Over the Diplomatic Security radio net came the chilling call: "We're under attack." A mile away at the CIA

Annex, the Global Response Staff (GRS) team heard the distress call and began preparing to respond.

At the compound, armed militants forced their way through the gates with AK-47s and rocket-propelled grenades. The local Libyan guards—lightly equipped and unable to resist effectively—offered little defense. Inside Villa C, Diplomatic Security Agent Scott Wickland stayed with Ambassador Stevens and Information Management Officer Sean Smith, ushering them into a secure area and barricading the door.

Attackers soon set fire to Villa C. Thick smoke filled the rooms, making it nearly impossible to breathe or see. Wickland later described struggling to lead Stevens and Smith to safety through the inferno before being forced to escape through a window.

By the time the GRS team from the Annex arrived, shortly after 10:00 p.m., Sean Smith was already dead from smoke inhalation. Ambassador Stevens could not be located in the darkness and smoke. Survivors regrouped and eventually withdrew to the CIA Annex before midnight.

In the early hours of September 12, at 5:15 a.m., militants launched a coordinated mortar attack on the Annex. Three rounds scored direct hits, killing Tyrone Woods and Glen Doherty, both former Navy SEALs working as security contractors.

By 6:00 a.m., reinforcements from the Libyan militia February 17 Brigade helped escort the remaining Americans to Benghazi airport. From there, US personnel, well and wounded and dead alike, were flown out of the city.[34]

Four Americans went home in body bags, including Ambassador Stevens, Sean Smith, Tyrone Woods, and Glen Doherty. Woods had served with SEAL Team Six. Doherty was a seasoned combat veteran. Both had survived Iraq and Afghanistan only to be killed on a rooftop in Benghazi as CIA contractors, abandoned by their own government.

What happened in Benghazi was a tragedy. What happened in Washington afterward was a cover-up. And it changed the course of American history.

The Benghazi attack didn't just expose the State Department's failures—it blew the lid off a covert CIA presence that almost no one outside the intelligence world knew existed. Officially, the facility just a mile from the consulate (Temporary Mission Facility) appeared to be part of the US diplomatic footprint. In reality, it housed CIA officers and contractors running classified operations—tracking local militant groups, monitoring the flow of weapons in post-Gaddafi Libya, and more than likely facilitating covert transfers to Syrian rebels—Obama's next failed regime-change experiment.

The CIA's presence and mission in Benghazi were so sensitive that even many members of Congress were unaware of the details. In the immediate aftermath of the attack, media outlets described the facility housing CIA personnel in vague terms—calling it a "safe house" or simply part of the US mission. Early reporting by *Reuters* repeatedly used the phrase "safe house," underscoring the ambiguity with which the annex was publicly characterized.[35]

But once the truth surfaced, it became clear that Benghazi was not just a tragic security disaster—it was the flashpoint for Obama's foreign policy failure, the moment when his reckless regime-change vanity projects in the Middle East were first laid bare.

The Obama administration denied that the CIA's Benghazi annex was involved in transferring arms to Syrian rebels. Yet as early as June 21, 2012, *The New York Times* had reported that "a small number of C.I.A. officers are operating secretly in southern Turkey, helping allies decide which Syrian opposition fighters across the border will receive arms to fight the Syrian government."[36]

On October 25, 2012, Fox News reported that a Libyan ship, allegedly carrying weapons bound for Syrian rebels, "may have some link" to the September 11 Benghazi attack. The vessel had docked in a Turkish port about thirty-five miles from the Syrian border, just five days before the assault that killed Ambassador Chris Stevens and three other Americans.[37]

That same evening, Stevens held what became his final official engagement: a meeting with Turkish Consul General Ali Sait Akin. Shortly before the attack began, around 9:35 p.m. local time, Stevens walked Akin to the front gate of the mission as he departed. The timing of that meeting has fueled lingering questions: What, exactly, was discussed?

Three days after the Benghazi attack, on September 14, 2012, *The Times of London* reported that "a Libyan ship carrying the largest consignment of weapons for Syria since the uprising began has docked in Turkey and most of its cargo is making its way to rebels on the front lines." Abu Muhammed, a member of the Free Syrian Army who helped move the cargo, told the *Times*: "This is the largest single delivery of assistance to the rebel fighting units we have received."[38]

A Libyan arms shipment bound for Syria, facilitated by Turkey; CIA involvement in monitoring weapons flows; and America's ambassador in Benghazi meeting with Turkey's top diplomat on the very night of the attack. Coincidence?

From the outset, the US "diplomatic presence" in Benghazi made little sense. Libya's official US Embassy was in Tripoli, the nation's capital. Yet, in 2011, the State Department established what was called the "Temporary Mission Facility" in Benghazi. It was not a full consulate, nor did it have the security infrastructure of a permanent embassy compound. Even the State Department's own Accountability Review Board later noted that the facility's defenses were inadequate: Its walls were easy to scale, barriers were minimal, and security relied heavily on local militias whose loyalties were questionable at best.

Given those realities, it was puzzling that Ambassador Stevens chose to be in Benghazi on September 11, 2012—a date that already carried high security sensitivity—to host meetings with foreign officials. Logic would suggest that such diplomacy would have been conducted in Tripoli, where the official embassy compound was located and where layered security was at least more substantial. Yet instead, Stevens met with Turkish Consul General Ali Sait Akin in Benghazi where his own staff admitted he would be "dangerously exposed."

Why was the ambassador in Benghazi at all, and why would he receive a senior Turkish diplomat there rather than in Tripoli? Those questions have never been fully answered. What is clear is that the choice of location made little strategic or security sense—unless, of course, the so-called "Temporary Mission Facility" in Benghazi functioned less as a diplomatic outpost and more as a convenient cover for the CIA annex operating just down the road.

We know that the Obama administration armed Syrian rebels through the CIA's covert program, Timber Sycamore—a multibillion-dollar operation run with the help of Saudi Arabia, Qatar, Turkey, and Jordan. Though publicly framed as support for "moderate" opposition, in practice many of the weapons ended up in the hands of jihadist factions, including al-Nusra, al-Qaeda's affiliate in Syria. It echoed the pattern in Libya, where

US and allied support for anti-Gaddafi forces had similarly empowered Islamist militias.

The Obama administration—and later even the House Intelligence Committee's investigation—insisted there was no evidence that the CIA annex in Benghazi had been involved in moving weapons to Syria. Officially, the annex was limited to intelligence collection and security support, but that denial has always strained credulity. The CIA had dozens of personnel on the ground in Benghazi, a city awash in unsecured arms after Gaddafi's fall. At the same time, Washington was running Timber Sycamore, the largest covert weapons program in its history, to funnel arms to anti-Assad rebels. To claim that the annex's proximity, timing, and manpower were unrelated to those transfers defies logic.

It was scandalous enough that jihadists in Benghazi carried out a successful, premeditated terrorist attack that left four Americans dead. But the tragedy was compounded by the fact that their deaths were not random—they were the direct consequence of Barack Obama's disastrous foreign policy. By toppling regimes, destabilizing entire nations, and funneling weapons into the hands of radical Islamists, his administration created the chaos in which America's enemies thrived. The Benghazi attack was not an isolated incident. It was the predictable outcome of a reckless strategy that empowered jihadists across the Middle East and North Africa while leaving American diplomats and security personnel fatally exposed.

If Obama had been using the CIA presence in Benghazi to funnel weapons from Libya into Syria, the revelation would have been politically devastating. In the middle of a reelection campaign built on the claim that he had ended wars and decimated al-Qaeda, proof that his administration was secretly arming

Islamist fighters would have been a death knell. It would have shattered the narrative of competence and restraint his White House had carefully cultivated, exposing instead another reckless, covert war.

The annex in Benghazi was not simply a "safe house," as the administration tried to suggest after the attack. It was more than likely part of a pipeline moving arms out of Libya and into the hands of Islamist fighters in Syria, continuing a pattern of dangerous policies that armed America's enemies under the guise of advancing democracy. Thus, the UK's *Telegraph* could confidently report on August 1, 2013 that the CIA's facility was an operation "to supply missiles from Libyan armouries to Syrian rebels."[39]

Benghazi was not just a tragedy—it was the deadly result of Obama's secret wars in Libya and Syria. The existence of the covert operation was only revealed because of the September 11, 2012 assault, after which leaks, investigative reporting, and congressional hearings revealed that the majority of Americans on the ground that night were CIA personnel, not State Department staff, and that the annex maintained its own quick reaction force, the Global Response Staff (GRS), which raced to the consulate to defend the Mission facility.

Keeping that role under wraps was politically vital for the Obama administration not only to protect ongoing operations, but to shield the White House from questions about whether those activities had contributed to the risk that led to the attack in the first place.

Picture yourself as Barack Obama on September 11, 2012. You're running for reelection with less than eight weeks until November 6. Despite the media myth that you are a once-in-a-generation, wildly popular, Messianic leader, the numbers tell a different story. Heading into September, you're clinging to a 1.6-point lead over Mitt Romney—at least, that's the average of fifteen national polls conducted in late August. How will you secure the win?

It's September 11, so your schedule for the day revolves around commemorating the eleventh anniversary of the attacks. It's probably your least favorite day of the year because you're forced to spend it doing your least favorite thing in the world—acknowledging an Islamic terrorist attack, the worst one in American history.

You appear on the South Lawn of the White House with the First Lady and your staff that morning to observe a moment of silence to mark the anniversary. Later, you travel with the First Lady to attend the 9/11 Observance Ceremony at the Pentagon. In the afternoon, you travel to Walter Reed National Military Medical Center and visit with representatives of the Wounded Warrior Project. The visit is closed to the press.[40]

By 5:00 p.m., you're back in the Oval Office preparing for a scheduled meeting with Secretary of Defense Leon Panetta.[41] Only ten weeks earlier, Panetta had been running the CIA, overseeing its role in the NATO-led operation that toppled Muammar Gaddafi. Under his tenure, the Agency established the Benghazi Annex in late 2011 as a base for intelligence operations and for monitoring the massive flow of weapons—some of which, according to multiple reports, were funneled toward Syrian rebel groups. Now, as secretary of defense, Panetta carries a dual burden: responsibility for the deteriorating conditions that had taken root in Libya, and responsibility for the US military response once those conditions exploded into violence.

And you—you're still Obama—have a scheduled meeting with Panetta at 5:00 p.m. Maybe you're already in the meeting or preparing for that meeting. In walks National Security Advisor Tom Donilon, your top aide on foreign policy and national security.[42] He delivers the news with the gravity the moment demands: "Mr. President…." Fill in the blank. What do you imagine he says? Do you think he tells you, as the administration would later claim, "Mr. President, a spontaneous protest broke out in Benghazi an hour and twenty minutes ago over an anti-Islam YouTube video, and the diplomatic compound housing the US Ambassador is under assault"? Of course not. There was no protest. There was no mob with signs and chants. There was only a well-coordinated jihadist attack underway against US personnel in Libya.

Minutes later—or perhaps you're already in their presence—you walk into your meeting with Panetta and Chairman of the Joint Chiefs of Staff General Martin Dempsey, the two men responsible for directing the US military response to the assault on Americans in Libya. You are briefed on the situation and give a single, vague directive: "Do whatever you need to do to be able to protect our people there."[43] After that, Panetta and Dempsey said, they had no further direct communication with the president that night. That's the official story anyway.

What else was said in that room, only the men present will ever know. But one thing is certain: Obama's bad day—spent reluctantly acknowledging Islamic terrorism on its anniversary—had just become a terrible, horrible, no good, very bad day.

Faced with deteriorating popularity and the consequences of being held accountable at the ballot box for your catastrophic decisions, what would you do? This is the reality of the situation Obama found himself in before he went to bed on the night of September 11, 2012. The stakes were nothing less than his re-election. And because Obama was willing to lie whenever necessary, the path forward was obvious. Instead of confronting the failure, he would construct a narrative—quickly, aggressively, and absolutely—that shifted blame, obscured responsibility, and protected his political survival at all costs.

The president knew instantly what the Benghazi attack meant. This wasn't just a tragedy; Americans were dead. It was a major foreign policy failure in a country his own administration had destabilized. Obama had approved airstrikes against Libya on March 19, 2011, destroying Gaddafi's air force and assets. He had authorized covert CIA operations to arm, train, and support Libyan rebels. He had told the world it was "not in our national interest" to let Gaddafi remain in power, warning that inaction would "[stain] the conscience of the world."[44] When Gaddafi was killed, Obama declared from the Rose Garden that "we achieved our objectives."

Only three days earlier, he had bragged in his weekly address about killing Osama bin Laden and putting al-Qaeda on the path to defeat. Yet in reality, the CIA was running a covert operation through Benghazi, facilitating weapons shipments from Libya's unsecured stockpiles, routed through intermediaries like Qatar, into the hands of Syrian rebels fighting Bashar al-Assad. Many of those fighters were hardline Islamists. The pipeline ran through Benghazi, where a CIA annex—just a mile from the doomed diplomatic compound—was central to the effort. The same foreign policy that armed Libyan militias to topple Gaddafi in 2011 was now arming Syrian factions in 2012, and Benghazi threatened to blow the lid off the entire operation.

Suddenly, the president was drowning in the knowledge of just how many scandals could erupt if Benghazi was scrutinized too closely. The attack risked exposing covert arms trafficking, a crumbling Libya, a resurgent al-Qaeda, and a reckless foreign policy sold to Americans as "success." Any one of these revelations could prove politically fatal. With less than eight weeks until Election Day, Obama needed to smother the story, control the narrative, and make sure the spotlight never lingered long enough to reveal the truths he could not afford to let the public see.

CHAPTER THREE

THE CLINTON SCANDAL THAT WASN'T

Many people, when they hear the word "Benghazi," instinctively associate it with Hillary Clinton. *Oh, the Clinton scandal,* they think. And they're not wrong. She was the secretary of state when the Benghazi attack took place, and it was her department that repeatedly ignored or denied requests by US Ambassador Chris Stevens and others to provide additional security and other defenses that could have prevented the massacre.

It was Obama's delusional foreign policy that turned Benghazi into a haven for radical Islamist terrorists. Still, Benghazi may very well have remained a Clinton scandal were it not for the decision made in the immediate aftermath to manufacture a false narrative using twelve-times revised CIA talking points that blamed the attack on a "spontaneous protest" sparked by an obscure anti-Islam YouTube video. The actions taken by the Obama administration in the week and a half or so after the September 11 attack would change the course of American history.

The attack was neither spontaneous nor sparked by a YouTube video. It was premeditated and carried out by al-Qaeda–affiliated terrorists. And the CIA, State Department, and White House knew it.

Within an hour of the first gunshots in Benghazi, a US drone had been redirected over the city. The Predator UAV started streaming live video of the attack back to Washington at 5:10 p.m. eastern time. That's 11:10 p.m. Benghazi time. The attack reportedly started at 9:42 p.m. Benghazi time. So both the initial assault on the diplomatic compound and the later mortar attack on the CIA Annex were recorded as they happened.[45]

For hours, the camera captured the chaos—fires engulfing the compound, armed militants swarming through the gates, defenders scrambling for cover. The feed was available to senior officials at the Pentagon, the State Department, and inside the White House Situation Room.

But reality contradicted the narrative President Obama had been selling to the American people—*al-Qaeda is on the run, and the world is safer than ever with President Obama in charge!* This delusion collapsed the moment heavily armed jihadists stormed the US diplomatic outpost in Benghazi. Rather than acknowledge what had happened and simply tell the truth, a decision was made to frame the attack as a spontaneous protest over a YouTube video—to tell a boldfaced lie. The decision was entirely political. Who gave the direction to push the lie wouldn't be known until April 18, 2014, nearly nineteen months later.

Secretary of State Clinton knew the Benghazi attack had been carried out by "an al-Qaeda-like group" the very day it happened. Just hours after the assault, she sent an email to "Diane

Reynolds"—an alias she used to communicate privately with her daughter Chelsea—that read: "Two of our officers were killed in Benghazi by an al-Qaeda-like group."[46] The revelation that "Diane Reynolds" was actually Chelsea Clinton only came to light in 2015 during the investigation into Hillary's secret private email server, but the duplicity was evident from the start.

Within twenty-four hours, she confidentially told Egyptian Prime Minister Hesham Kandil that the attack "had nothing to do with the film" and was instead "a planned attack—not a protest."[47] Two days after the attack, Sidney Blumenthal, Hillary's former campaign advisor, Clinton family lackey, and longtime friend, sent her an email citing sensitive sources that said the attacks "had been planned for approximately one month" and carried out by "well-trained, hardened killers" from Ansar al-Sharia, the Libyan al-Qaeda affiliated terrorist group.[48] Clinton knew the truth—even admitted it in private—and yet publicly pushed a very different story.

At 10:08 p.m. on the night of the attack, Clinton issued her first public statement suggesting that the violence was triggered by an anti-Islam YouTube video, declaring, "Some have sought to justify this vicious behavior as a response to inflammatory material posted on the Internet."

To be fair, such a video did exist. An Egyptian-born Coptic Christian living in California, Nakoula Basseley Nakoula, had uploaded a fourteen-minute trailer for a low-budget, anti-Islam film back in July 2012. While it had absolutely nothing to do with what happened in Benghazi, protests did break out in Cairo on September 11 over the video. Titled *The Innocence of Muslims*, the footage had been shot in California in 2011 with amateur actors in front of green screens. In post-production, Nakoula dubbed the dialogue to depict Muhammad as a murderous, lecherous fraud and his followers as violent and depraved. Nakoula was no Egyptian Tarantino, so nobody noticed the film at first—until another Egyptian-born Coptic Christian in the US, Morris Sadek, reposted the trailer on his blog in early September and blasted the link to dozens of journalists. Arabic-language media in Egypt quickly picked it up, and within days, satellite channels were looping a dubbed version while Islamist commentators denounced it as a grave insult to the Prophet Muhammad.[49]

Groups of the so-called peaceful, nonviolent Muslims took to the streets in Cairo and gathered outside the US embassy, where they proceeded to chant anti-American slogans, throw rocks and Molotov cocktails toward the compound, and scale the embassy's outer wall. Once inside, they pulled down the American flag, shredded it, and replaced it with a black banner similar to those used by the jihadist groups. No American personnel were injured, and Egyptian security forces eventually dispersed the crowd.

The fact that there actually was a spontaneous protest in Cairo over an offensive YouTube video on the very same day that armed jihadists murdered four Americans in Benghazi made Obama's cover story even more incredulous. The Cairo protests provided a benchmark of comparison. Do participants in a "spontaneous protest"—a sudden, unplanned gathering—arrive under cover of darkness after daytime surveillance, armed with AK-47s, RPGs, mortars, hand grenades, gallons of diesel fuel, and heavy machine guns mounted on trucks, and then execute a coordinated assault that leaves four Americans dead? No. That is not a protest. That is a premeditated terrorist attack.

Furthermore, Cairo isn't in Libya—it's in Egypt. A different country entirely. The notion that a few hours of protests in Cairo could, on the same night, spontaneously trigger a coordinated, multi-hour paramilitary assault in Benghazi is as absurd as suggesting that a riot in Paris could instantly set off a paramilitary operation in Munich.

The entire premise that the Benghazi terrorist attack was merely a spontaneous protest sparked by an offensive video made by a US-based Egyptian Coptic Christian was an insult to human intelligence. Any additional intelligence confirming the indisputable fact that it was a premeditated Islamist terrorist attack was almost superfluous. On the very morning of the attack, Ambassador Chris Stevens had sent a three-page cable to the State Department describing a city spiraling out of control. He reported that Libyan security forces had been infiltrated by extremist militias, that law and order had effectively collapsed, and that the US compound itself was under surveillance.

According to Stevens, a man in a Libyan police uniform had been spotted on the upper floor of a nearby building that was under construction, photographing the inside of the compound with a cell phone. Letters collected at the consulate after the attack corroborated this. More than six weeks after the attack, reporters found a draft letter intended for the head of the Libyan Ministry of Foreign Affairs in Benghazi:

> …[E]arly this morning at 0643, September 11, 2012, one of our diligent guards made a troubling report. Near our main gate, a member of the police force was seen in the upper level of a building across from our compound. It is reported that this person was photographing the inside of the U.S. special mission and

furthermore that this person was part of the police unit sent to protect the mission.[50]

The FBI had conducted its own on-site investigation nearly a month prior.

Another draft letter dated two days before the attack complained that requested local police support for Ambassador's visit hadn't been provided.

> …We requested daily, twenty-four hour police protection at the front and rear of the U.S. mission as well as a roving patrol. In addition we requested the services of a police explosive detection dog. We were given assurances from the highest authorities in the Ministry of Foreign Affairs that all due support would be provided for Ambassador Stevens' visit to Benghazi. However, we are saddened to report that we have only received an occasional police presence at our main gate. Many hours pass when we have no police support at all.[51]

Ambassador Stevens had raised similar concerns to the State Department that summer, warning that both the local police and the February 17 Martyrs Brigade—the militia contracted to guard the mission—were unreliable, often absent from their posts, and in some cases suspected of colluding with extremist elements.

What happened in Benghazi was as obvious as what had happened at Fort Hood, when a Muslim US Army Major—who had been communicating with al-Qaeda's top recruiter for over a year—jumped onto a table shouting "Allahu Akbar" and opened fire. But America's first Muslim president didn't see it that way. Obama's modus operandi was to twist himself into a pretzel to deny the obvious—and it was an election year. Not just any election year, but less than two months before voters went to the polls. To acknowledge what had truly happened in Benghazi would have exposed the dangerous and disastrous consequences of his foreign policy in Libya and across the Middle East, shattering the illusion that his administration was winning the war on radical Islam. And so the White House manufactured the Benghazi hoax.

Though this flimsy narrative unraveled within a week of its introduction, the deeper scandal wouldn't come to light until nearly twenty months later. On September 14, 2012, three days after the attack, the CIA drafted talking points for lawmakers and administration officials ahead of Sunday television appearances. That Friday draft then went through twelve revisions before being handed to Susan Rice, the US ambassador to the United Nations. That Sunday, Rice appeared on five major political talk shows, insisting that the attacks appeared to be the result of a spontaneous protest over an anti-Islam video rather than a planned terrorist assault.

But why Susan Rice? Why was the US ambassador to the UN chosen as the administration's public face instead of Secretary of State Hillary Clinton? One would think the secretary of state—the top official responsible for the very department under attack—would be sent out to explain Benghazi to the American people. Instead, the White House deployed Rice, a diplomatic second-stringer. It was like sending the cheerleading director of an NFL team to face the media after a Super Bowl blowout instead of the head coach. The administration's excuse? Clinton was "unavailable" that day.

No doubt she was. After all, she was the boss of the State Department—the part of the government in charge of the people who died—so people would have asked her hard questions which might have caused trouble for her later. Instead, the administration sent someone else, Susan Rice, who wasn't directly in charge. That way, Hillary didn't have to answer the tough questions, and if anything went wrong, it wouldn't land on her.

We know that Susan Rice was lying on behalf of the Obama administration because Secretary of State Clinton had been told by longtime confidant Sidney Blumenthal that the attacks had been planned for a month and carried out by Ansar al-Sharia. Even before that, she had told her daughter that an "al-Qaeda-like"—in other words, an affiliated group—had done it.

It was a cover-up to influence the 2016 election and help reelect the Administrative Mafia's preferred candidate, Barack Hussein Obama. The intelligence community—in this case, the CIA—made this possible.

Obama had already worked with intelligence agencies, including both the FBI and Pentagon, to effectively bury the truth about the Fort Hood shooting, ensuring it was officially labeled "workplace violence" rather than the jihadist act that it was. He would do it again with Benghazi—with one significant difference.

After Fort Hood, the US Government did not manufacture intelligence to mislead the American public about what actually happened. This time, the CIA would revise its talking points a staggering twelve times, at the direction of the White House, stripping out references to al-Qaeda, prior security warnings, and the premeditated nature of the assault, with the *intent* of selling the American people a lie.

ABC News's Jonathan Karl published a devastating exposé on May 10, 2013—conveniently, after Obama had secured reelection. In it, he revealed how the Benghazi talking points morphed from a blunt acknowledgment of a premeditated terrorist strike into a sanitized narrative about a spontaneous protest. The initial CIA draft, circulated on September 14, 2012, explicitly stated that "Islamic extremists with ties to al-Qa'ida participated in the attack" and referenced prior surveillance of US facilities as well as earlier incidents in Benghazi, including attacks on foreign interests and British diplomatic convoys. The original draft described exactly what happened.[52]

But the State Department intervened. Spokeswoman Victoria Nuland objected to the language, warning in one email that the paragraph "could be abused by members [of Congress] to beat up the State Department for not paying attention to warnings," and asked why they would want to "feed that either." She later pressed that the revised versions "didn't resolve all of my issues" and demanded further deletions. Notice the mindset: Nuland wasn't treating the CIA as an independent intelligence agency but as a political instrument to be managed. Her concerns weren't about whether the CIA's initial assessment was accurate—it was—but about how those facts might be used politically against the State Department.

The final version of the talking points that was cleared through a White House "Deputies Committee" stripped all references to terrorism, al-Qaeda, and prior warning signals per Nuland and the Obama administration's request. That version was the one publicly delivered by Ambassador Rice on five Sunday talk shows, where she portrayed the incident as a spontaneous reaction to an anti-Islam video.

Karl's reporting provided the first public evidence that the talking points were politically scrubbed to protect the Obama administration's image. But Karl quickly found himself in the crosshairs of the Obama White House because one email he referenced from Deputy National Security Advisor for Strategic Communications and Speechwriting Ben Rhodes turned out to be misquoted. A confidential source—still not identified—had given Karl a paraphrased or summarized internal White House email. Karl had never seen the actual email, and he presented the content as a direct quote.

In Karl's words:

> In an email dated 9/14/12 at 9:34 p.m.—three days after the attack and two days before Ambassador Rice appeared on the Sunday shows—Deputy National Security Advisor Ben Rhodes wrote an email saying the State Department's concerns needed to be addressed.
>
> "We must make sure that the talking points reflect all agency equities, including those of the State Department, and we don't want to undermine the FBI investigation. We thus will work through the talking points tomorrow morning at the Deputies Committee meeting.[53]

Karl was claiming this White House email from Ben Rhodes showed the talking points were edited to protect the State Department. Within three days, CNN's Jake Tapper obtained the actual email, revealing that Rhodes never mentioned the State Department. The actual quote stated: "We need to resolve this in a way that respects all of the relevant equities, particularly the investigation."

Ironically, as we would later learn, the actual Rhodes email was probably more damning than Karl's inaccurate quote. The misquote led Karl to conclude that the Obama administration wanted to make sure the revised talking points protected the State Department. Rhodes's actual email that made no reference to the State Department implied that the Obama administration wanted to make sure the revised talking points protected Obama. But at the time, this deeper implication was completely missed. No one realized that the administration's real priority wasn't shielding Foggy Bottom—it was shielding the president. The purpose of providing Jake Tapper with the actual Rhodes' email was simply to discredit Karl and that was achieved.

Both alternatives—the Karl misquoted email and Rhodes' actual email—were scandalous. But the matter rose to an impeachable offense if the president of the United States, through Ben Rhodes or anyone else in his inner circle, personally directed the CIA to manipulate intelligence with the intent of shielding Obama from political damage less than two months out from an election.

At the time, even eight months after the attack, the accepted wisdom was that the botched Benghazi cover-up was a State Department mess. No one yet realized it was Obama and his inner circle who had ordered the CIA's talking points to be rewritten to mislead the public about what happened in Benghazi.

The reason the White House and media were really outraged over Jonathan Karl's misquote of the Rhodes email was not because of any moral qualms over journalistic malpractice, but because Karl had unwittingly tied the cover-up to Obama. Ben Rhodes didn't work for the State Department—his title was deputy national security advisor for strategic communications in the Obama White House. That meant he was essentially Obama's chief foreign policy message-crafter, responsible for shaping the administration's public narrative on national security and foreign affairs—including Benghazi. Both Rhodes's misquoted summary of an email *and* the actual email provided to Tapper provided a paper trail that led to the Oval Office.

Jonathan Karl was over the target. And for that, he had to pay the price. The media quickly discredited and humiliated him, branding his scoop "sloppy journalism" and "inaccurate reporting." Tom Fiedler, dean at Boston University's College of Communication, accused Karl of being "sloppy—or being deliberately ambiguous—about these e-mails…to enhance the 'exclusive' he claimed to have." Kevin Smith, chair of the Society of Professional Journalists Ethics Committee, dismissed it as "inaccurate reporting," faulting Karl for presenting summaries as direct quotes.[54] At a White House press briefing, spokesman Jay Carney seized the moment, telling reporters it was proof of Republicans' willingness to "cherry pick information, or in this case, make it up in order to fit a political narrative."[55]

The White House strategy worked. Attention shifted away from Karl's underlying revelation—that Obama's inner circle had ordered the CIA, a supposedly independent intelligence agency, to falsify its own assessment to protect the president during an election year. Instead, the story became about Karl's sourcing. A chilling message was also sent to journalists like Karl, who dared engage in an act of actual journalism that sought to expose Obama corruption: the truth would be punished, the process would be attacked, and anyone who scrutinized the narrative would be professionally destroyed.

Obama was subsequently recast as the victim, Republicans were painted as dishonest partisans willing to "make things up," and the media eagerly amplified the distraction. The real scandal—how the Benghazi talking points were politically scrubbed to help Obama win reelection—was buried beneath a manufactured scandal about a reporter's quotation marks.

CHAPTER FOUR

OBAMA–MEDIA COLLUSION: THE CURIOUS CASE OF THE MISSING DAVID LETTERMAN INTERVIEW

n his Rose Garden remarks on September 12, 2012—the day after the Benghazi attack—President Obama refused to call what had transpired an act of Islamic terrorism. He first described it as "an attack on our diplomatic outpost in Benghazi," then as "an outrageous and shocking attack." True to form, he did not break his golden rule and used the occasion to defend Islam in the aftermath of an Islamist attack, declaring, "We reject all efforts to denigrate the religious beliefs of others." As he wrapped up his address, he offered only a vague line: "No acts of terror will ever shake the resolve of this great nation." Obama routinely employed the phrase "act of terror" as a rhetorical escape hatch without ever naming Islamic terrorism directly, a verbal sleight of hand to deflect from politically inconvenient truths.[56]

A notable exception to Obama's willful vagueness came after the San Bernardino, California attack, carried out by Syed Rizwan Farook, a US-born Muslim, and his Pakistani-born wife, Tashfeen Malik. The pair pledged allegiance to the Islamic State on social media before killing fourteen people and wounding twenty-two more at a county health department holiday gathering. Days later, the FBI announced it was investigating the massacre as an act of terrorism—and Obama quickly adopted the FBI's language, calling it an "act of terrorism" in a nationally televised Oval Office address.[57] The fact that Obama did, in this case, use the term "act of terrorism" shows he understood the distinction between a nonspecific label like "terror"—which could apply to any violent crime or mass shooting—and the specific designation "terrorism," which carried a political and ideological implication.

In Benghazi, Obama made a deliberate political choice to avoid the word "terrorism." He settled instead for the generic "act of terror," the old rhetorical sleight of hand. Even so, an "act of terror" is not the same thing as a "spontaneous protest." But this was only one day after the attack, and the White House had not yet fully hatched the Benghazi hoax. It wasn't polished, Obama-approved, and ready for prime time until the evening of September 15, 2012, three full days after the attack. That night, the final version of the CIA's talking points—now scrubbed of every reference to al-Qaeda, Islamic extremism, and prior security warnings—was circulated among senior administration officials.

CIA Deputy Director Mike Morell personally oversaw these edits, narrowing the language to fit the White House's preferred "spontaneous protest" narrative. He deleted language stating, "There are indications that Islamic extremists participated in the violent demonstrations," along with references to prior warnings from the Cairo embassy and intelligence suggesting the attack was premeditated.[58]

Morell knowingly falsified intelligence to bail out the Obama White House in the final stretch of the 2012 presidential campaign, acting less like the deputy director of the CIA than a political fixer for the Administrative Mafia's preferred candidate. And it wouldn't be the last time. Eight years later, in 2020, Morell reprised the role—this time as a former intelligence official—by orchestrating the now-infamous letter signed by fifty-one former intelligence operatives claiming, without evidence, that the Hunter Biden laptop story had "all the classic earmarks of Russian disinformation." His was the fifty-first signature, the final stamp of approval on another intelligence-backed political deception.

Of all the former intelligence officials still operating in Washington in 2020, it was Morell whom Biden campaign advisor Antony Blinken called on to recruit signatories. Morell later admitted under oath that his decision to take on the task was "triggered" by two things: Blinken's outreach and his personal desire to help Joe Biden in the debate and to "win the election."[59] This cockroach was the consummate Washington, Deep State fixer. If you're looking for a face to attach to the swamp, Morell is it.

His mild, forgettable exterior—neatly parted hair, wire-rimmed glasses, the demeanor of a CPA—was the perfect camouflage for one of Washington's most loyal liars. Over three decades inside the CIA, he briefed George W. Bush on 9/11, helped shape intelligence for the Iraq War, and later became Obama's deputy CIA director, mastering the bureaucratic art of shaping intelligence to fit political needs. When he left government, Morell didn't vanish—he slipped through the revolving door into Beacon Global Strategies, a lobbying powerhouse stacked with national security insiders, while also securing a perch at CBS News as a "national security analyst" to shape public perception.

In any case, just days after Susan Rice made her rounds on the Sunday shows parroting the Obama–Morell "spontaneous protest" hoax, President Obama himself went on the *Late Show with David Letterman* on September 18 and doubled down. "Extremists and terrorists used [the video] as an excuse to attack a variety of our embassies, including the consulate in Libya," Obama said.[60]

The narrative was now drifting into even more absurd territory. Rice had dutifully told America that Benghazi was the product of a "spontaneous protest" over an anti-Islam YouTube video. But Obama now claimed terrorists had simply used the video as an excuse. Which was it—spontaneous or preplanned? And since when do terrorists need an excuse? Was Obama really suggesting that jihadists had been sitting in their living rooms for months, AK-47s at the ready, praying for the day some Egyptian-born Coptic Christian in California would upload a video mocking Muhammad so they could finally have a pretext to slaughter Americans in Benghazi?

It was a humiliating and scandalous statement. Republican presidential nominee Mitt Romney could have and should have run campaign ads in all fifty states utilizing that clip of Obama blaming the attack on a video.

The hoax was collapsing under the weight of its own absurdity, common sense, and an ongoing investigation by the Senate Homeland Security and Governmental Affairs Committee. Chaired by Senator Joe Lieberman with Senator Susan Collins as ranking member, the committee had launched its inquiry within days of the attack, requesting briefings and documents from the State Department and intelligence agencies.

In fact, the day after Obama told Letterman that the Benghazi attackers had used the anti-Islam YouTube video as an "excuse," Matthew Olsen, director of the National Counterterrorism Center, testified before the Senate Homeland Security Committee and formally admitted that "[t]hey [the Benghazi victims] were killed in the course of a terrorist attack on our embassy."[61] In other words, a YouTube video had nothing to do with it.

But something curious happened between the time that Obama told Letterman that a YouTube video was responsible for the attack and Olsen's testimony the following day admitting that a YouTube video wasn't responsible for the attack. These were the headlines covering the Obama interview on Letterman:

> *The Washington Post*: "On Letterman, Obama says Romney 'writing off' much of country."[62]

> *Los Angeles Times*: "Obama Responds to Romney Remarks in David Letterman Interview."[63]

> *CBS News:* "President Addresses Controversial Romney Comments During Sit-Down With Letterman."[64]

> *NBC News:* "Obama slams Romney on Letterman for 'writing off a big chunk of the country'"

The Wall Street Journal: "On 'Letterman,' Obama
Responds to Romney's '47 Percent' Remarks"

Every one of those headlines should have read: "Obama repeats debunked Benghazi Hoax on 'Letterman.'"

Both the official CBS News and the David Letterman YouTube pages feature countless short clips and even full interviews from past shows during his long tenure as the late-night host. CBS News even has two short clips from Obama's September 18, 2012 appearance available—one in which the president and Letterman joke about seeing the host naked, and another in which Obama sharply criticizes his opponent, Mitt Romney, for the infamous "47 percent" comment.

But what's not available is the most historically relevant portion of the interview: the exact moment President Obama blamed the Benghazi attack on a YouTube video. That moment appears to be the only time Obama personally and publicly endorsed the hoax that he had helped create, and it inexplicably vanished from the record.

The media never reported on it, even while they reported on Obama's *Letterman* appearance. It was quietly, deliberately memory-holed, as if it had never happened.

Not only is that clip not available on CBS News's YouTube— it's not available anywhere on YouTube, or elsewhere. But at one point, it was.

On September 19, 2012, a YouTube account named Lex Luger uploaded the full Obama–Letterman interview. *Time Magazine* even embedded Luger's video in its coverage of the appearance: "Obama on Letterman: Top 10 Things You Missed If You Didn't Watch Last Night." By September 27, the video had racked up more than 165,000 views. The account itself wasn't prolific—Lex Luger had posted only twelve videos in total. All of this is verifiable through archived snapshots on the Internet Archive's Wayback Machine, which lets users see exactly what a webpage looked like on a given date, even if it has since been altered or deleted. But the Wayback Machine doesn't capture everything—it only takes periodic snapshots. And the next snapshot, dated October 7, 2012, tells the story. Poof. The video was gone. Not taken down by its uploader, not quietly aged out of relevance—*disappeared.*

The YouTube account hosting the video was terminated "due to multiple third-party notifications of copyright infringement" sometime between September 27 and October 7. In other words, the one piece of undeniable, concrete evidence showing the president of the United States personally promoting the Benghazi hoax vanished from public view, erasing the chance for Americans to watch it and judge for themselves.

Maybe it was just a coincidence. Maybe Lex Luger had bad luck. Out of all the countless other users who uploaded full interviews, short clips, and even entire episodes of *The Late Show*, his channel—of all of them—was the one taken down. You can go on YouTube right now and spend weeks watching past *Letterman* interviews with presidents, movie stars, athletes, comedians, and musicians. Entire episodes have been preserved by third-party users and remain readily available. But not this one. Not the September 18, 2012, interview with Barack Obama—where, at a critical moment in the Benghazi fallout, the president himself blamed the attack on an anti-Islam video.

The Washington Post even posted a link to Obama's full interview: "Video: Obama's full interview on the 'Late Show with David Letterman.'"[65] The link is still there today, but click it, and you're greeted with a blank page stamped with "404 Not Found."[66]

Amid the mysterious disappearances, one thing is evident: There was a coordinated effort to suppress Obama's September 18 *Letterman* appearance, where the president personally advanced the Benghazi hoax by blaming the attack on a YouTube video.

Just days before Obama's *Letterman* appearance, *Mother Jones* released a secretly recorded video from a private Romney fundraiser in May, four months earlier, in which Romney remarked that "47 percent of the people" were Obama supporters dependent on government who saw themselves as victims.[67] During the *Letterman* taping, Obama was asked to address the video. That clip of Obama "slamming" Romney—as media outlets breathlessly described it—is still on YouTube, CBS News's own site, and countless other outlets. The third-party accounts that uploaded *that* clip are still alive and well. Their accounts haven't been terminated. That's the clip CBS and Obama were happy to see survive, the one they rubber-stamped as "safe." That's the clip Lex Luger should have posted if he wanted to dodge the censors.

Notably, Obama mentioned the video again two days after the *Letterman* appearance at the Univision Townhall on September 20, 2012. But he did not explicitly blame the Benghazi attack on the video, as he had done on *Letterman*. "What we do know is that the natural protests that arose because of the outrage over the video were used as an excuse by extremists to see if they can also directly harm U.S. interests," he said during the townhall.[68]

Obama's September 20 Univision appearance is his last known public mention of the anti-Islam video in connection to the Benghazi attack. After that, the administration's messaging shifted entirely. Intelligence reports and subsequent internal findings clearly framed the assault as a planned terrorist operation, not a spontaneous reaction to protest.

Obama's *Letterman* appearance explicitly linking the YouTube video to the Benghazi attack should have been politically fatal. It was proof that the president of the United States—not some staffer or Susan Rice—was knowingly misleading the country to protect his reelection storyline that al-Qaeda was "on the run."

In the days that followed Obama's *Letterman* appearance, not a single reporter asked the president to explain why he had personally tied the Benghazi attack to a YouTube video—a claim his own intelligence agencies had already debunked. Nor did a single member of the press corps question White House Press Secretary Jay Carney about it in any of the daily briefings on September 19, 20, or 21—or at any point thereafter. The most directly incriminating statement Obama ever made on Benghazi simply vanished from the media's collective memory.

The best—and perhaps only—opportunity to break through the media blackout and expose Obama's role in the Benghazi hoax as an active participant, not a passive bystander, came weeks later at the second presidential debate at Hofstra University. It was October 16, a town hall–style debate where the candidates moved freely around the stage and took questions from undecided voters. The moderator was CNN's Candy Crowley, whose role in the evening would prove anything but neutral. The format gave her unusual latitude to intervene, and she quickly revealed herself less as a moderator than as Obama's onstage ally and babysitter, ready to step in when the president faltered. Romney's opening to land a knockout blow finally arrived when a woman in the audience asked Obama directly why the State Department had denied enhanced security for the embassy in Benghazi.

Not surprisingly, Obama dodged the question. Instead, he offered his usual vague platitudes about the bravery of America's diplomats and the need to "get to the bottom" of what happened—before pivoting to accuse Romney of politicizing Benghazi. Outrageously, Obama even claimed he had immediately ordered a full investigation "regardless of where the facts lead us." But the reality was the opposite: He had ordered the CIA to ignore the facts, cover up what happened, and lie. Obama was the one who politicized Benghazi, and the singular figure who most needed to be held accountable was Obama himself. Romney was the only man on that stage who had the chance to do it.

Romney got his chance to respond, but instead of going straight for the jugular, he danced and jabbed. "There was no demonstration involved," he said. "It was a terrorist attack, and it took a long time for that to be told to the American people.... Whether there was some misleading, or instead whether we just didn't know what happened, you have to ask yourself why didn't we know five days later when the ambassador to the United Nations went on TV to say that this was a demonstration?"[69] Romney was getting closer, but he never delivered the fatal blow. All he needed to say was: "Mr. President, you personally went on the *Late Show with David Letterman* on September 18 and blamed Benghazi on a YouTube video. You misled the American people with full knowledge that it was a premeditated terrorist attack. Why did you lie? Will you admit here and now that it was a terrorist attack carried out by radical Islamist extremists?"

Instead, Romney kept circling: "We've read eyewitness accounts now about what happened. It was very clear this was not a demonstration. This was an attack by terrorists." The stage was set. Obama, visibly cornered, tried to flip the script: "The day after the attack, governor, I stood in the Rose Garden and

I told the American people that this was an act of terror." Then he gaslit Romney: "And the suggestion that anybody in my team would play politics or mislead when we've lost four of our own, governor, is offensive. That's not what we do. That's not what I do as president, that's not what I do as Commander in Chief."[70]

The moment was ripe for Romney. He began to press: "I think it's interesting the president just said…that on the day after the attack he went into the Rose Garden and said this was an act of terror. You said it was an act of terror, not a spontaneous demonstration—is that what you're saying?" "That's what I said," Obama replied. "Please proceed, governor." Romney pushed: "I want to make sure we get that for the record, because it took the president 14 days before he called Benghazi an act of terror." Obama smirked: "Get the transcript." And then came the infamous Candy Crowley moment. Before Romney could finish, Crowley jumped in to bail Obama out: "He did in fact call it an act of terror." Obama seized it instantly, turning to her with a grin: "Can you say that a little louder, Candy?" "He did call it an act of terror," Crowley repeated for the national audience.

In that instant, the moderator stopped being a neutral referee and became Obama's fact-checker, freezing Romney's momentum and giving Obama a priceless assist. Romney tried to clarify: "The administration indicated this was a reaction to a video and was a spontaneous reaction." But the damage was done. Millions of viewers were left with the false impression that Obama's account had been consistent from day one. Romney had whiffed. The knockout blow was right there—Obama's *Letterman* appearance was the smoking gun—but Romney never threw the punch.

Still, there are important takeaways from that debate. At the critical moment when Romney could have landed a fatal political blow, he whiffed because of a semantic mistake. In the context of the exchange, it was clear what Romney meant—Obama hadn't called Benghazi an act of terrorism. Romney had already laid out the point earlier: "…[T]here was no demonstration involved," he said. "It was a terrorist attack and it took a long time for that to be told to the American people." Romney's real aim was to challenge Obama on the delay—to force him to explain why, in the days after the attack, his administration kept blaming a YouTube video instead of telling the truth. But instead of framing the exchange around the false narrative, Romney zeroed in on whether Obama had used a particular phrase in the Rose Garden—and botched it.[71]

That seemingly minor mistake opened the door for Obama to claim a semantic victory and for Crowley to play referee, transforming what could have been a devastating moment into a controversy that worked in Obama's favor. Republicans were outraged at Crowley's obvious bias and interference, rightly so. Democrats spun the exchange into proof that Obama had been "consistent all along." And the real scandal—Obama's personal involvement in repeating the YouTube lie—was buried. His *Letterman* appearance linking Benghazi to the video, a full week after the attack, vanished beneath the manufactured triumph of the "act of terror" soundbite.

After the debate, Crowley admitted what millions of viewers never heard that night—that Romney was "right in the main."[72] Obama had indeed uttered the phrase "acts of terror" in the Rose Garden, but Romney's broader point was correct: In the days that followed, the administration repeatedly and deliberately pushed the false narrative that Benghazi was sparked by a protest over a YouTube video, rather than a preplanned terrorist assault. By the time she walked it back, the damage to Romney was done—and the media had already banked the clip as a victory for Obama.

Another important takeaway from the Hofstra debate is how, when Obama found himself up against the ropes, he instinctively turned to the referee for rescue. That reflex is, in many ways, the most scandalous part of the exchange: The president of the United States, in the middle of a high-stakes debate over a national security disaster, expected the moderator to save him. Obama narrowly escaped the most dangerous moment of his political campaign with the assistance of a complicit media, a partisan CNN debate moderator, and a poorly timed misstep by Romney.

The final presidential debate took place a week later at Lynn University in Boca Raton, Florida. Despite its focus on foreign policy—arguably Obama's greatest political vulnerability—he managed to reframe his record as a success. One moment from that night, however, would stand out above all others. Standing on stage, Obama mocked Romney for calling Russia America's greatest geopolitical foe. Delivering a line that drew applause in the hall and was replayed endlessly in the press, he sneered: "Governor Romney, I'm glad that you recognize that al Qaeda is a threat, because a few months ago when you were asked what's the biggest geopolitical threat facing America, you said Russia, not al Qaeda; you said Russia. And the 1980s are now calling to ask for their foreign policy back, because, you know, the Cold War's been over for 20 years."[73]

Unfortunately, Candy Crowley wasn't there to fact-check Obama. Romney had, in fact, used the word "foe," not "threat," when describing Russia. But Obama's "zinger" wouldn't age well. Four years later, Russia was no longer a punchline—it was elevated by Obama himself into the role of dangerous geopolitical villain.

In December 2016, he stood before the nation and declared that Russia had interfered in the election to help elect Donald Trump, transforming the very country he once mocked as irrelevant into the centerpiece of a political narrative that would dominate—and distort—American politics for years to come.

Nevertheless, Obama went on to win the 2012 presidential election.

Victoria Nuland, the State Department's spokesperson, appeared before the Senate Homeland Security Committee on September 19, 2012, the day after Obama's outrageous *Letterman* claim. Under oath, she told senators that the administration "stood by" the intelligence community's judgment that it was a terrorist event.[74]

Was this the same woman who, just days earlier, had been helping to scrub the CIA's talking points of any reference to terrorism, al-Qaeda, or prior security warnings? The same Nuland who, in internal email traffic, objected to language that might "be abused by Members of Congress" looking to hold the State Department accountable?

Nor was she the only official to admit knowledge of the truth. National Counterterrorism Center Director Matthew Olsen said plainly it was "a terrorist attack." Secretary of State Hillary Clinton, who publicly addressed the Benghazi attack in a written statement on September 11, 2012 and made her first on-camera appearance on September 12, went into hiding afterwards only to reemerge on September 21, 2012, to say, "What happened in Benghazi was a terrorist attack, and we will not rest until we have tracked down and brought to justice the terrorists who murdered four Americans."[75]

On September 25, 2012—two full weeks after the Benghazi attack—Obama appeared on *The View* and still refused to call it a terrorist attack outright. "We're still doing an investigation," he told the hosts.[76] By that point, intelligence reports had long since concluded it was a coordinated terrorist assault, yet Obama continued to publicly downplay the reality. It was the same playbook he had used after the Fort Hood massacre: deny, deflect, and delay—anything to avoid admitting the obvious truth about Islamic terrorism.

Was Nuland fired? Prosecuted? Of course not. Instead, she was rewarded. She was moved from her post as State Department spokesperson to assistant secretary of state for European and Eurasian affairs, where she oversaw US policy toward Europe, Russia, and Central Asia in Obama's second term. Later, she resurfaced in the Biden administration as under secretary of state for political affairs—the third-highest position in the State Department, responsible for directing US diplomatic strategy worldwide. Nuland is a career diplomat who also served under George W. Bush as US ambassador to NATO. In other words, she's not a partisan outsider—she's a permanent fixture. Another card-carrying member of the Deep State and Administrative Mafia.

They have names. Like Mike Morell. Victoria Nuland. They're not lurking in the shadows; they're hiding in plain sight, moving seamlessly from one administration to the next, shaping policy and narratives regardless of whoever the voters send to the White House.

The anti-Islam video narrative was a hoax—a sloppy but highly coordinated effort to meddle in the 2012 presidential election to sway it in Obama's favor. It involved the CIA, the State Department, Secretary of State Hillary Clinton, President Obama, and others.

Not a single person involved in the election year Benghazi cover-up was ever held accountable. No one was fired. No one was prosecuted. Four years later, Hillary Clinton would become the Democratic nominee for president.

I imagine many Americans have moved on from Benghazi. To them, it was just another tragic event, one of the countless scandals the Administrative Mafia has gotten away with. It happened nearly fifteen years ago, and they assume it has no relevance today. But I disagree. Benghazi led directly to Trump–Russia collusion, which led to the rigged 2020 election, which led to the unprecedented lawfare leading up to the 2024 election.

Why do Democrats and the Administrative Mafia hate Donald Trump more than any other Republican candidate in modern American history? Why did they go to such extraordinary and lawless lengths to try to stop him from winning in 2016—and then expose themselves in a desperate attempt to drive him from office? What was it about that election that drove Obama and Hillary Clinton to brazenly weaponize the intelligence community against a political opponent?

The similarities between the Trump–Russia collusion hoax and the Benghazi scandal are impossible to ignore. In 2012, Obama was running for reelection on the claim that his administration had decimated al-Qaeda and stabilized the Middle East. The terrorist attack in Benghazi shattered that narrative. Instead of telling the truth—that four Americans had been murdered in a premeditated assault by Islamic extremists—the Obama administration, aided by Clinton, the CIA, and others, built a politically convenient fiction: that a "spontaneous protest" over a YouTube video had gotten out of hand. The goal was simple— protect Obama's image and survive Election Day.

Four years later, the same playbook was dusted off. Only this time, the stakes were higher—and the target was Donald Trump. But before we turn to that, Benghazi's story still isn't finished.

CHAPTER FIVE

BENGHAZI'S REVENGE

President Obama won reelection in 2012 and escaped the Benghazi scandal relatively unscathed. Despite the deaths of four Americans and the rush of negative publicity, the controversy didn't cost him the White House. The media moved on. The public, for the most part, followed. But Benghazi wasn't extinct—it was simply dormant. A Freedom of Information Act (FOIA) lawsuit filed by Judicial Watch on December 19, 2012, was the spark that relit the fuse that would eventually blow the real scandal wide open.[77]

After the State Department failed to respond to Judicial Watch's December 19, 2012 FOIA request, the group sued in federal court in early 2013 to compel the release of Benghazi records—a litigation campaign that produced additional suits and document releases through 2014.[78]

It took nearly sixteen months from the initial FOIA request for the State Department to turn over the Ben Rhodes email, which was released in April 2014 only after a federal judge forced their hand. For well over a year, the administration slow-walked, stonewalled, and withheld records that should have been produced within weeks under the law. Buried in those pages was a previously hidden email from Ben Rhodes, deputy national security advisor to President Obama. That single email was a bombshell, and the dormant Benghazi scandal exploded back into public view. This scandal was even bigger than the last.

It started when Congress asked President Obama's team for all the papers about Benghazi. Obama's team gave them some papers and made Congress think that was everything. But it wasn't. They kept the most important paper hidden for almost two years.

In 2012 and 2013, multiple committees—including Oversight, Intelligence, Foreign Affairs, and Armed Services—issued subpoenas and formal requests for every scrap of paper related to the attack. The Obama administration responded with large batches of records, representing them as "responsive" and "complete." Lawmakers proceeded under the assumption that nothing was being withheld. Even official committee reports were built on that false premise, with no hint that key documents were missing.

In the real world, knowingly hiding subpoenaed evidence is a crime; in Washington, it's a political strategy. In the real world, people go to prison. In Washington, they don't even lose their jobs. Consider Martha Stewart, who was prosecuted and convicted in 2004 not for the stock trade she arranged, but for misleading federal investigators afterward. She concealed key information, made false statements, and as a result spent five months in federal prison.

Now compare that to the Obama administration's handling of the Ben Rhodes email. Congress lawfully demanded all Benghazi-related records, and the White House assured lawmakers they had turned everything over. In reality, one of the most politically damaging documents was deliberately withheld for nearly two years and only surfaced after a federal judge forced its release. The conduct—concealing evidence and misleading investigators—was essentially the same. The difference? Stewart was an ordinary citizen, so she went to prison. Obama's team was the government, so it got away with it.

Federal prosecutors went after Stewart with unusual zeal, in part because she was one of the most famous business figures in America. Convicting her gave the government a high-profile "teachable moment"—proof that even the rich and powerful could be punished for lying to investigators. But the same logic that drove prosecutors to make an example out of Stewart should apply tenfold to government officials—especially those involved in a cover-up on the scale of Benghazi. If the goal is to deter dishonesty and abuse of power, then refusing to hold officials accountable sends the opposite message: that the level of corruption an Obama administration official can get away with is limited only by the boundaries of their imagination.

The previously hidden Rhodes email, dated September 14, 2012, carried the subject line: "RE: PREP CALL with Susan, Saturday at 4:00 pm ET." The "prep" referred to Susan Rice's Sunday show appearances to discuss Benghazi. In the email, Rhodes advised that the "goal" was to "underscore that these protests are rooted in an Internet video, and not a broader failure of policy."[79]

Why did this matter? Hadn't earlier investigations—including Jonathan Karl's ABC News exposé of May 10, 2013—already revealed that the Obama administration and CIA had misled the American people about Benghazi? Not quite. Karl's story collapsed under media outrage when it turned out he had misquoted a different Rhodes email. But the outrage wasn't really about journalistic precision—it was about protecting Obama. Karl's version suggested the White House itself was directing the cover-up to protect Hillary Clinton and the State Department. That subtle difference mattered enormously. If Karl had been right, it wouldn't just have been a Clinton scandal—it would have been an Obama scandal. Without realizing it, Karl had wandered too close to the truth.

And that's what made the September 14 email explosive. It wasn't so much the content—by then, everyone knew the "video" narrative was false. It was the author and the timing. Ben Rhodes was no low-level staffer. He was the deputy national security advisor for strategic communications—a senior official in the Obama White House with direct access to the president. Which meant this wasn't a bureaucratic talking point shuffled around between the CIA and State. It was a political directive from the West Wing. From Obama.

The email was sent on September 14, 2012—a Friday. Rice didn't go on TV until Sunday.

Even though it was widely understood that Barack Obama was the ultimate beneficiary of the Benghazi cover story, there was no "smoking gun" document or recorded order that directly linked him to the edits in the CIA talking points. That's how Washington works. Presidents don't send emails that say "change the intel to help my campaign." They have layers—chiefs of staff, national security advisors, communications directors—who "coordinate" decisions that just happen to align perfectly with the president's political needs.

By the time an order filters down to the CIA or the State Department, it comes from a committee, not from the Oval Office. The House Select Committee on Benghazi documented that the changes to the talking points were made through a

White House Deputies Committee process that included the president's closest advisors.

The fingerprints of others were everywhere, while the president's own hands remained clean. But in Washington, the absence of a signed confession isn't proof of innocence; it's proof of how well the operation was run. The talking points were gutted of references to al-Qaeda, and the false narrative was pushed on national television in the heat of an election. Whether Obama gave the order verbally in the Situation Room or simply nodded while his staff carried it out, the result was the same: The intelligence community's assessment was rewritten to protect his reelection campaign.

The scandals multiplied like Russian nesting dolls—open one, and inside were two more, and inside those four more, and so on. Each cover-up spawned its own scandal. First, there was the State Department scandal—four Americans died on Hillary Clinton's watch, the product of gross negligence and ignored warnings. Then came the second scandal—Obama's choice to invent a narrative blaming the attack on spontaneous protests triggered by an obscure YouTube video. Then a third—the deliberate withholding of documents from Congress that revealed the White House's direct role in shaping that lie.

None of this would have happened if the Obama White House hadn't politicized the CIA and ordered Mike Morell to corrupt the intelligence. But once they did, the dominoes began to fall. And in the process, something else was exposed—something the White House never intended to see the light of day. That was Hillary Clinton's secret private email server.

It had been in both Obama's and Clinton's political interest to contain the fallout, but their interests weren't identical. Clinton wanted to save face, protect her reputation, and preserve her chances for a future presidential run. Obama's presidency itself was on the line. In the middle of a reelection campaign, he could have let Clinton fall on the sword and blamed her instead of a video. He could have fired people, scapegoated subordinates, and let the outrage land squarely at the State Department's feet. But that wouldn't have solved Obama's problem.

Obama had built his reelection campaign around the claim that terrorism was in retreat and that the world was safer thanks to his leadership. He had boasted of al-Qaeda's decline, of Osama bin Laden's death, and of Gaddafi's fall—his proud, public initiatives. To admit that al-Qaeda-linked militants had carried out a coordinated assault on a US diplomatic outpost on the anniversary of 9/11 would have obliterated that illusion just weeks before Americans went to the polls. It was a risk he wasn't willing to take. And in the end, the gamble paid off. He kept the lie alive long enough to win. He was still president.

Moving forward, it's important to understand that there were no longer distinct Clinton scandals and Obama scandals. By this point, the lines had blurred. The so-called Deep State— the Administrative Mafia—was a fully operational, well-oiled machine. Clinton and Obama were political bedfellows, bound together by shared interests and shared cover-ups. Protecting power came first; truth, law, and accountability came last, if at all. The Obama White House was not merely complicit—it was poisonous, infecting the entire government with corruption and rot.

The House Select Committee on Benghazi was established on May 8, 2014, to reexamine what earlier investigations had missed—particularly in light of newly "discovered" documents that had been withheld from Congress. The most explosive revelation came ten months later with the discovery of Hillary Clinton's private email server. This was not just another twist in the Benghazi scandal. It was an altogether new scandal, one that reached all the way to the president of the United States. On March 2, 2015, *The New York Times* broke the story with the headline: "Hillary Clinton Used Personal Email Account at State Dept., Possibly Breaking Rules."[80]

At the time, Hillary Clinton was secretary of state, one of the top jobs in the US government. She was supposed to use official government email accounts so her messages were archived, secure, and available for oversight—especially when national security was involved. But Clinton didn't do that. Instead, she used her own private email server, set up at her house, to send and receive all her government emails. That meant her messages were outside the government system and couldn't be accessed through normal channels like FOIA requests or congressional subpoenas.

This became a huge problem during the Benghazi investigation. When investigators asked for Hillary Clinton's emails, they discovered she hadn't been using an official account at all—and that tens of thousands of messages had already been deleted. Her team insisted they were merely "personal," but because they weren't stored on government servers, no one could verify that claim. The scandal, therefore, wasn't just about emails. It was about breaking federal rules, evading transparency, and possibly destroying public records, all while under investigation for a deadly attack on Americans overseas.

It's hard to overstate how insane this was. Hillary Clinton officially left the Obama administration on February 1, 2013. She spent the next year raking in nearly $10 million in paid speeches—including $1.6 million from major Wall Street banks—while laying the groundwork for her 2016 presidential run.[81] In 2014, she published *Hard Choices*, her obligatory pre-campaign memoir. Everyone in Washington knew what was coming.

Then, in the summer of 2014, while Clinton was cashing checks and polishing her image, the House Select Committee on Benghazi requested documents and communications from the State Department, including Clinton's emails from her time as secretary of state. That's when the State Department realized it didn't have them. Why? Because Clinton had used a private server for her entire tenure.

So in late October 2014, the State Department asked Clinton's lawyers to turn over her emails. Over the next month, her team unilaterally reviewed the contents of her private server—without any government oversight—and made their own judgment calls on what was "work-related" and what was "personal." On December 5, 2014, they turned over 30,490 emails they deemed government-related. But outrageously, they had already deleted 31,830 others—nearly half—on the claim they were "personal," erasing them before the government ever saw them.[82]

Three months later, on March 2, 2015, *The New York Times* broke the story. Only then did the American public learn that Hillary Clinton had used a secret, home-based server for all of her government business—and had already destroyed half the record. This destruction was professional. It wasn't just dragging files into the little trash can at the bottom of the computer screen and clicking "empty." Clinton's team used BleachBit, a digital shredding tool, to permanently erase the emails, overwrite the data, and ensure the contents could never be recovered, even by forensic experts. It was the digital equivalent of tossing thousands of pages of evidence into a burning barrel and dousing them with gasoline.

Clinton clearly wanted to guarantee that no one—Congress, the FBI, or the American people—would ever see what was in those emails. And crucially, she didn't delete them upon leaving office. She deleted them after being asked to preserve them—after they were subpoenaed. That distinction matters because by the time her team ran BleachBit, her records were already under subpoena. In any other context, this would not be called "deleting emails." It would be called destroying evidence.

So now we have a new scandal. And let's be honest—"scandal" is just a placeholder word for a crime that you can't call a crime. Because every time a member of the Administrative Mafia commits one, the system refuses to bring charges or put them in prison. If I drive eighty miles an hour in a thirty zone, texting while not wearing a seatbelt, and a cop pulls me over but lets me off with a warning—did I still commit a crime? Of course I did. How about if I tell the officer, "I didn't intend to speed"? Does that get me off the hook?

In early July 2015, inspectors general from the State Department and the Intelligence Community formally referred concerns about Hillary Clinton's private email server to the Federal Bureau of Investigation. On July 10, 2015, the FBI opened a criminal investigation into whether classified information had been mishandled, improperly stored, or destroyed—not a "security review," as Clinton publicly claimed.[83]

But before we even get into the crimes—plural—let's just deal with the first and most obvious one of using a private server. What is a private server?

It's not just a personal email address. It's a separate, privately run email system physically installed in Hillary Clinton's home in Chappaqua, New York, operating completely outside secure government networks. It was hidden from the State Department's

IT infrastructure and wasn't subject to the normal archiving, security, or oversight protocols required by federal law.

As secretary of state, Hillary Clinton was legally required to follow the Federal Records Act, which mandates that all official communications be preserved and available to the agency and to the National Archives. But Clinton's private server was never authorized, never secured by the US government, and never subject to proper archiving procedures. It operated entirely illegally.

She also violated State Department regulations, which made it clear that employees must use authorized, secure government systems, especially when handling sensitive or classified material. Her private server had no legal clearance for classified information, yet more than one hundred classified emails, including some marked top secret, were later discovered on it.

One of the main reasons federal officials are required to use government-secured email systems is to protect against foreign hackers and espionage. Government servers are monitored, encrypted, and hardened against cyberattacks. Personal servers are not. By using a secret, unsecured server in her basement, Hillary Clinton exposed sensitive government communications to foreign intelligence services.

And this wasn't just a hypothetical risk. The FBI concluded that Clinton's server was targeted by foreign actors and likely compromised. In Director James Comey's own words, "We assess it is possible that hostile actors gained access."[84] She was emailing classified information, including top secret intelligence, on a system that lacked even the basic protections required by law.

A lot of people get lost in the weeds when it comes to "private email" versus "private server." And that's not by accident—it's been deliberately muddied by defenders of Hillary Clinton. Here's the truth: Using a private email account is not the same as using a private server. Lots of government officials have, at times, used personal email accounts (like Gmail or Yahoo) to send messages. That's still a violation of federal record-keeping rules if used for official business, but those emails are stored on third-party servers owned and operated by companies like Google or Microsoft. With Gmail, for example, the government can subpoena Google and get your emails.

Clinton didn't just use a personal email account—she ran her own private server. That means she (and her team) controlled the entire system: the hardware, the storage, the security (or lack of it), and the data access. It wasn't hosted by Google, Yahoo, or any other platform. It was a custom-built email system, physically installed in her home, completely outside the oversight of the federal government.

No Cabinet-level official is supposed to set up their own secret communications system. But Clinton did it from the very beginning of her tenure as secretary of state, and no one stopped her. The server was registered the same week she took office in 2009.[85] She never used a State.gov email address—not once. And while a few close aides and IT staff knew about the private server, top officials at the State Department's IT, legal, and security divisions were never informed.

There was no approval, no security audit, no compliance check. It wasn't authorized because she never asked for authorization—she just did it. And because she was Hillary Clinton, no one dared to challenge her. The result? An illegal, unmonitored, and unsecured private email system operated in secret for four years at the highest levels of the US government—until the public found out too late.

But that's not all. Anyone in government who ever emailed Hillary Clinton—or received an email from her—knew without question that she wasn't using a government-issued State.gov address. There was no confusion. Her email—hdr22@clintonemail.com—was clearly a personal account. It wasn't a secret. It was obvious. No one said a word because they were either complicit, willfully blind, or understood the unspoken rule in Washington: You don't question powerful people—especially not Hillary Clinton, the presumed future first female president.

President Obama was asked about Hillary Clinton's private email use in a sit-down interview with CBS News's Bill Plante on March 7, 2015—just days after *The New York Times* broke the story. Plante asked, "Mr. President, when did you first learn that Hillary Clinton used an email system outside the U.S. government for official business while she was Secretary of State?"

Obama replied, "The same time everybody else learned it—through news reports."[86]

Obviously, the president of the United States would have exchanged emails with his secretary of state. And since she didn't use a state.gov email address, he would have been emailing her at hdr22@clintonemail.com—obviously a private email address! Obama lied. Another scandal was revealed, and another cover-up was underway.

Clinton's emails were gone for good, even those that landed in the president's inbox. When a president sends an email to someone using a private, non-government account, only the outgoing message is automatically archived under the Presidential Records Act (PRA), which governs the preservation of presidential communications.[87] The recipient's reply—unless it is forwarded to or sent through an official government system—is not captured.

In Hillary Clinton's case, her use of a private server meant that her replies to President Obama were never stored in official government archives. Federal law and amendments passed in 2014 require officials to ensure any work-related personal emails are properly preserved.[88] Since Clinton deleted over thirty thousand messages she claimed were personal, many of her communications with the president may have been permanently lost, leaving critical gaps in the legal and historical record.

This scandal had national security implications. It wasn't just that Clinton and Obama made a mistake or were even deliberately trying to conceal communications. It was that they knowingly conducted official government business over an unsecured, unauthorized system—outside federal oversight—while handling information that could have included classified or sensitive material. By bypassing secure channels, they exposed the highest levels of American diplomacy to potential foreign surveillance, undermined transparency, and violated the very protocols meant to protect national interests. And as we will later discover, the Russians had hacked the Obama administration.

Obama had repeatedly claimed that he would lead "the most transparent administration in history." He first made this pledge during his 2008 presidential campaign. He reaffirmed it after taking office. "My Administration is committed to creating an unprecedented level of openness in government," President Obama wrote in a White House memo on Transparency and Open Government on January 21, 2009.[89]

Despite the likely preservation of Obama's own communications with Clinton during the Benghazi investigation, Clinton's side of the exchange was never archived by the State Department or made available to Congress or investigators. In other words, when she deleted more than thirty thousand emails she unilaterally deemed "personal," she may have effectively erased part of the official record. A black hole in the paper trail was created at the center of one of the most politically explosive episodes of Obama's entire presidency.

The president's emails are some of the hardest government records to access. They're protected by the Presidential Records Act, and many of them are also shielded by executive privilege, which lets the White House keep certain communications secret, especially those related to national security or sensitive decisions. That means even if Congress or investigators want to see a president's emails, they usually can't get them without a court order or special permission. In most cases, these records are locked away for twelve years after a president leaves office. It's a system designed to protect the presidency, but it also makes it very hard to hold a president accountable in a situation like this one.[90] Had Hillary Clinton not deleted more than thirty thousand emails from her private server, a full investigation might have revealed criminal violations—potentially both by her and by President Obama.

Clinton's use of a private server to conduct all official business as secretary of state was a clear violation of the Federal Records Act. But more than that, over one hundred classified emails—including some marked top secret—were found on her server, raising serious questions about mishandling of classified material, a felony under the Espionage Act (18 US Code § 793).

Her team's use of BleachBit to irreversibly erase emails after a congressional subpoena had been issued could also constitute obstruction of justice (18 US Code § 1519). If she coordinated the deletion of those records with others, it could rise to criminal conspiracy (18 US Code § 371).

For President Obama, legal exposure would hinge on what he knew and when. If it were shown that Obama knowingly allowed Clinton to bypass record keeping laws, concealed it, or misled investigators, he could have been implicated in conspiracy or making false statements. Furthermore, if classified material was exchanged between them through her private server, it raised national security concerns. Because Clinton deleted the emails, we may never know the full extent of the lawbreaking. But make no mistake: The cover-up protected not just Hillary Clinton—it also protected the president of the United States.

There are many inflection points in America's history, as there are in our own lives. But without question, the terrorist attack that claimed the lives of four Americans in Benghazi on September 11, 2012, set in motion a chain of events that ushered in an era of political depravity and destruction from which America has yet to recover. The Big Bang in Benghazi gave birth to entire galaxies of corruption. And it bound together the unlikely pair of Barack Obama and Hillary Clinton in a political suicide pact, each clutching secrets that could destroy them both.

Benghazi would grow into the Trump–Russia collusion hoax, and the coconspirators would utilize every dirty tactic they'd rehearsed throughout the Obama administration to pull it off. It was political guerrilla warfare, and nobody saw it coming.

CHAPTER SIX

THE PROBLEM WITH THE PREMISE

The Clinton campaign alleged that Republican presidential candidate Donald J. Trump was "colluding" with Vladimir Putin to interfere in the 2016 presidential election to help him beat Democrat presidential candidate Hillary Rodham Clinton. That's the gist of the allegation at the center of the Trump–Russia hoax.

Did Democrats see in Trump's actions a scandal similar to how Obama colluded with the CIA and the media during his 2012 reelection campaign? Is that what they meant by "collusion," even if they refused to admit the resemblance?

In fact, Trump did not collude with the Russians to win the election. The supposed Trump–Russia collusion was the Benghazi hoax 2.0. The main difference between the Benghazi hoax and the Trump–Russia collusion hoax is that the Benghazi hoax wasn't created to destroy Obama's political opponent Mitt

Romney. That was a desperate reflex designed to cover up a tragic and inconvenient event that made Obama look bad and threatened to sink his campaign. When Benghazi happened, the election was less than eight weeks away. It had a short runway. Obama won his reelection, and the problem was solved.

The Trump–Russia collusion, in contrast, was created by the Clinton team not only to distract from her email scandal, but to destroy her political opponent in an election year. Do you understand the difference? The Benghazi hoax was a defensive strategy. The Trump–Russia collusion was an offensive strategy.

The exact term "Trump–Russia collusion" didn't start circulating until the latter part of 2016, and it became mainstream in the early part of 2017 after Trump was elected. But before the Democrats gave their hoax a real name, it implied the same thing. The accusation was just "collusion" or "ties to Russia," a vague but politically charged accusation designed to plant suspicion in the minds of voters and set the stage for the narrative that would dominate the next four years and beyond.

While it was dangerous, far more than the Benghazi hoax, you had to be stupid to believe it. Lack of any credible, material evidence aside, you only had to answer one very simple question to see through it all: Would Russia be better off with Hillary Clinton as US president or Donald Trump?

When Barack Obama took office in 2009, one of his early foreign policy priorities was to improve relations with Russia. He believed that the icy post–Cold War dynamic could be "reset" through diplomacy and cooperation. His administration rolled out the initiative with fanfare, most famously when Hillary Clinton handed Russian Foreign Minister Sergey Lavrov a symbolic red "reset" button (mistranslated as "overcharge").[91]

The goal was to build trust with Moscow, work together on arms reduction, counterterrorism, and nuclear nonproliferation, and create a more stable US–Russia relationship.

In 2010, the Obama administration approved one of the most reckless national security decisions of the decade: allowing Rosatom, a Russian state-owned nuclear giant, to acquire a controlling stake in Uranium One. This was a Canadian firm that held mining stakes that totaled roughly 20 percent of America's uranium production capacity.

In plain terms, "production capacity" doesn't mean uranium already pulled from the ground—it means the ability to mine and process uranium in the future. Uranium One owned the mines and facilities that, if fully operated, could produce one-fifth of all the uranium America is capable of mining. That gave them strategic control. Put simply, it meant the Russians had leverage over the US nuclear fuel supply chain, even though the uranium could never legally leave US soil. Russia's control over the manufacturing process gave them long-term geopolitical power in future political or economic disputes.

Because uranium is a strategic resource for nuclear weapons and power production, the deal had to be cleared by the Committee on Foreign Investment in the United States, a panel that included Hillary Clinton's State Department. Several of Uranium One's owners were also donors to the Clinton Foundation, giving $145 million between them.[92] And in June 2010, while the deal was under review, Bill Clinton flew to Moscow to give a single speech. His fee? An eye-popping $500,000, paid by Renaissance Capital, a Kremlin-linked bank that was actively promoting Uranium One stock to investors.[93]

The conflict of interest was glaring. Hillary Clinton's department was weighing whether to approve the sale of a company controlling a fifth of America's uranium production capacity to Russia, while her husband pocketed half a million dollars from a bank with a direct stake in the deal. Worse, US officials already knew Russia was engaged in a bribery and kickback scheme tied to its nuclear expansion. Yet the deal went through anyway. Years later, Democrats would paint Russia as America's top geopolitical villain and smear Donald Trump as a Kremlin asset—conveniently forgetting that when they were in power, they had literally handed Vladimir Putin 20 percent of America's uranium capacity on a silver platter.

At the very moment the Uranium One deal was under review, there was an active FBI criminal investigation into Rosatom's US operations. Agents had uncovered evidence that the Russian nuclear giant was engaged in a wide-ranging bribery and money laundering scheme designed to expand Moscow's grip on America's uranium market. They had secured a confidential informant, recorded conversations, and compiled documents showing that Russian officials were using corrupt tactics to burrow their way into the US nuclear industry.[94]

In any normal context, such an investigation would have been a blaring red siren—the kind of intelligence that should have stopped cold any deal granting Moscow more control over American uranium. Instead, the probe was quietly buried while the Obama administration approved the Uranium One transaction. Neither Congress nor the public was informed that the buyer was already under criminal investigation.

Aside from this specific instance of pro-Russia pandering, there was also Obama's weak, America-last foreign policy—and by extension, Hillary Clinton's. From the failed "reset" with Moscow to his chronic reluctance to confront Russian aggression, Obama's foreign policy consistently played to the Kremlin's advantage. His administration pushed for the 2010 "reset" with Russia, softening America's posture just as Moscow was expanding its global influence.

In 2014, Russia annexed Crimea, and Obama offered little more than symbolic sanctions that failed to deter further aggression. And even earlier, in September 2009, Obama abruptly scrapped President George W. Bush's plan to deploy a missile defense shield in Poland and the Czech Republic—a system designed to guard against long-range missile threats from Iran but fiercely opposed by Moscow.[95]

Obama framed the reversal as part of his "reset," hoping for Russian cooperation on issues like Iran's nuclear program. But in Eastern Europe, the move was seen as a betrayal, especially since the announcement came on September 17, the seventieth anniversary of the Soviet invasion of Poland. For Russia, it was an unearned strategic victory, one that undermined US influence in the region and signaled to Vladimir Putin that this White House could be swayed by Kremlin pressure. From the start, Obama's foreign policy gestures gave Russia more than they got in return—a pattern that would repeat itself in far more consequential ways.

And who can forget that moment in the final 2012 presidential debate? Mitt Romney warned that Russia was America's "greatest geopolitical foe." Obama smirked and fired back with a line the media replayed endlessly: "The 1980s are now calling to ask for their foreign policy back, because the Cold War's been over for 20 years." The audience laughed, the press swooned, and Vladimir Putin smiled. Russia, according to Obama, was no longer an enemy worth worrying about. Less than four years later, that same president would stand before the American people and accuse Russia of interfering in the US election to help Donald Trump defeat Hillary Clinton.

So let me again pose the question: Would Vladimir Putin have been better off with a President Clinton or a President Trump? The entire Trump–Russia collusion narrative was every bit as unbelievable—and unbelievably stupid—as the Benghazi "spontaneous protest" hoax. The problem with both was the same: Reality stood in the way of what the Democrats wanted the public to believe. But there is another reason the collusion theory never passed the smell test, a reason rooted in how Washington worked long before Donald Trump ever came down the golden escalator.

For decades, Washington functioned according to a rigid hierarchy—an unspoken caste system where presidents come and go, but the establishment remains. This permanent ruling class, the unelected bureaucracy, the intelligence mandarins, the diplomatic lifers, the think-tank apparatchiks—*they* are the continuity of government. These are the Victoria Nulands, the Mike Morells, the John Brennans. They survive every administration and expect every new president to understand one thing: the system runs *them*, not the other way around.

Most Americans imagine a president as an all-powerful actor. Washington knows better. In the modern era, the president is expected to absorb the norms, defer to the experts, and become just another replaceable part of the Administrative Machine. That was the arrangement long before Trump—and it's why "change" never actually changes anything.

Then Trump showed up.

He didn't come from within their ranks. He didn't owe them anything. He didn't fear them. And he had no interest in learning "how things are done." That alone made him a threat—not because of Russia, but because he disrupted the cozy continuity the establishment had enjoyed for decades.

Which brings us back to the Russia hoax. The fact that every major figure pushing the collusion narrative just happened to be a loyal servant of the pre-Trump establishment—a collection of people who viewed Trump as an existential threat to their power—did not exactly inspire confidence. And then there was the most glaring problem of all: *reality*. If any American administration had given Vladimir Putin everything he could have dreamed of, it wasn't the Trump Administration. It was Barack Obama's—and Hillary Clinton's—policies that strengthened Russia, enriched Russia, and expanded Russia's ambitions.

CHAPTER SEVEN

POLITICAL SLEIGHT OF HAND

We know the Trump–Russia collusion was a load of BS for the same reason we know the Benghazi "spontaneous protest" was BS: one, facts, and two, more facts. Both were political cover stories manufactured in real time to shield Democrat presidential candidates from scandal. In Benghazi, the Obama administration spun a fairy tale about a YouTube video to conceal the reality of a coordinated terrorist attack on the anniversary of 9/11. Four years later, Hillary Clinton's campaign concocted the Trump–Russia hoax to shift blame from her very real email scandal onto her opponent, by inventing a scandal that was entirely fake. In both cases, the truth was obvious to anyone paying attention, and the timelines and internal communications of the hoax's architects prove they knew it was false from day one.

Let's briefly rewind the tape. In November 2012, Susan Rice, Obama's ambassador to the United Nations, was handed the dirty task of launching the Benghazi hoax. She went on five Sunday talk shows in a single morning, relentlessly pushing the false story that an obscure YouTube video had triggered a "spontaneous protest" which just happened to overrun a US diplomatic compound on the anniversary of 9/11. Four years later, in July 2016, Hillary Clinton's campaign manager, Robby Mook, played the role of hoax salesman.

Just two days earlier, WikiLeaks had dumped nearly twenty thousand internal DNC emails, showing party officials privately working to undermine Bernie Sanders during the Democratic primary—confirming for millions of voters that the process had been rigged behind the scenes to coronate Hillary Clinton as the nominee.. On the morning of July 24, 2016, when Mook appeared on CNN's *State of the Union*, Jake Tapper asked him: "What is the reaction of the Clinton campaign to these DNC leaked emails suggesting that top officials, including the CFO there, were actively discussing ways to hurt Bernie Sanders in the primaries?"

Mook didn't bother defending the DNC. Instead, he pivoted, replying: "What's disturbing to us is that we—experts are telling us that Russian state actors broke into the DNC, stole these emails. And other experts are now saying that the Russians are releasing these emails for the purpose of actually helping Donald Trump."[96]

Rather than address the content of the emails, Mook deflected, telling Jake Tapper that "experts" believed the leaks came from Russia and were intended to help Donald Trump. With that single statement, the Clinton campaign transformed a scandal about its own collusion and interference in the

Democratic primary into a narrative about foreign interference. The press ran with it immediately, echoing Mook's claim as if it were fact. What began as a public relations crisis for the Democrats was, within forty-eight hours, reframed into the storyline that would dominate American politics for years: the Trump–Russia collusion.

Conventional wisdom says the DNC leaks should have been a crippling blow to Hillary Clinton, perfectly timed to sow chaos as she prepared to accept the Democratic nomination. In truth, they saved her. For months, Clinton had been cornered by the email scandal—grilled over her reckless use of a private server, dragged before Congress, and branded in the public eye as corrupt and untrustworthy. Even though FBI Director James Comey publicly exonerated her on July 5, just weeks before the DNC, it did little to restore her credibility. Comey himself branded her "extremely careless" with classified information. She had committed crimes, lied about them repeatedly, and walked away unpunished.

For months on the campaign trail, she flatly denied ever sending or receiving classified emails. In March 2015, she told reporters at the United Nations: "I did not email any classified material to anyone. There is no classified material."[97] In July 2016 on NBC's *Meet the Press*, she repeated: "I never received nor sent any material that was marked classified."[98] Both statements were false. The FBI found 110 emails in fifty-two chains that contained classified information, including some marked top secret.[99]

To voters, she wasn't innocent—she was untouchable. The legal cloud may have lifted, but the political cloud remained, threatening to overshadow her nomination and follow her into November. The WikiLeaks dump gave her a lifeline. It was the best thing that could have happened to her. Instead of being the scandal-plagued candidate dodging accountability, she could now recast herself as the victim of a foreign plot. Almost overnight, the headlines shifted. They were no longer about Clinton's misconduct, but about Russia's supposed interference to help Trump. What should have been her campaign's death sentence became the perfect pretext for a new narrative—one that buried her crimes under the cover of a national security crisis.

It was political sleight of hand. Think of that iconic opening scene in *Raiders of the Lost Ark*, where Indiana Jones swaps the golden idol for a bag of sand. In an instant, the Clinton campaign pulled off the same trick. The "idol" was Clinton's email scandal—heavy, dangerous, and ready to crush her candidacy. The "sand" was the Trump–Russia collusion. With one quick pivot, her team swapped out the narrative: Instead of Clinton being judged for her own misconduct, the focus shifted to Russia allegedly attacking American democracy.

Despite the chorus of headlines declaring Russia as the culprit, no hard proof has ever been produced showing that WikiLeaks received the stolen emails from the Kremlin. The US intelligence community asserted this conclusion with "high confidence," but its case rested on inference, secret sourcing, and the work of CrowdStrike.

CrowdStrike was the cybersecurity firm the DNC hired instead of the FBI. Yet under oath, CrowdStrike president Shawn Henry admitted they could not prove the most essential point—that any data had actually been stolen. "There's circumstantial evidence, but no evidence that they were actually exfiltrated," Henry told Congress.[100] In plain English, CrowdStrike identified signs that the DNC network had been compromised, but it never produced forensic proof showing that the emails later published by WikiLeaks were actually copied from the DNC servers by an outside hacker. Despite this, the media and intelligence community confidently told the public that Russia had taken the emails, when the very company at the center of the claim could not prove it.

Julian Assange, the founder of WikiLeaks, flatly denied that the Russians were his source, insisting WikiLeaks had never received material from Moscow or any state actor.[101] Even Robert Mueller's sweeping report—while echoing the official line that Russian intelligence (the GRU) hacked the DNC and supplied the emails to WikiLeaks—failed to demonstrate a direct handoff between the GRU and Assange's organization.[102] The chain of custody remains a mystery. And the one fact that endures is this: The claim that "Russia gave the emails to WikiLeaks" has never been proven—only asserted.

It's the kind of claim that would struggle in court. Circumstantial evidence can support a case—but only if it proves the crime itself. Evidence of a possible intrusion is not proof that anything was actually stolen, and a judge would not allow a theft case to proceed without evidence that a theft occurred. Yet in the court of public opinion, that was enough. The media and the intelligence community treated CrowdStrike's guesswork as gospel, convicting Russia—and by extension, Trump—on evidence that wouldn't stand five minutes under cross-examination.

The Russians most likely did hack the DNC. There's ample evidence of that. The relevant question isn't whether Moscow gained access to DNC emails and internal communications—the question is whether they exfiltrated that data and handed it off to WikiLeaks. And that distinction matters. Hacking into a system is one thing; stealing data and supplying it to a third party for political sabotage is another. Yet the entire flimsy Trump–Russia collusion narrative launched by Clinton campaign advisor Robby Mook rested on that leap.

But let's just say, for the sake of argument, that it really was the Russians who passed those DNC emails to Julian Assange. This still doesn't change the core fact that it wasn't Russia that put them in front of the American people. It was Assange. He alone decided when and how to publish, timing the release to coincide with the DNC. That distinction matters. Clinton's campaign needed the story to be about Russia directly interfering in the election on Trump's behalf. But in reality, even if Moscow had been the source, the public release was Assange's call, not the Kremlin's.

The Clinton plan took it a step further. It wasn't enough to claim—without hard evidence—that Russia had hacked the DNC and handed the emails to WikiLeaks. They made an even bigger leap: that Vladimir Putin had done it with the specific motive of helping Donald Trump win the election. That claim wasn't just unproven—it was unknowable. Motive is the hardest thing to establish even in a courtroom with hard evidence, yet here it was simply invented out of thin air and repeated as fact. The irony, of course, is that Hillary Clinton herself had just been exonerated in the email scandal precisely because investigators claimed they couldn't prove intent. In her case, lack of demonstrable motive cleared her. In Trump's, a completely fabricated motive was enough to brand him a Russian asset.

The irony is hard to miss. Years before the DNC scandal, Julian Assange had already become infamous for unleashing the largest classified leaks in American history. In 2010, WikiLeaks published the *Afghan War Diary*, the *Iraq War Logs*, and *Cablegate*—hundreds of thousands of secret military and diplomatic documents that rocked Washington.[103] At the time,

Assange worked hand-in-glove with establishment outlets like *The New York Times* and *The Guardian*, who eagerly splashed his leaks across their front pages and celebrated him as a fearless crusader for transparency.

But when 2016 rolled around and WikiLeaks began releasing emails that embarrassed Democrats and Hillary Clinton, the same media that once embraced Assange turned on him. Overnight, he went from hero to villain not because he had changed his methods, but because he had targeted the wrong people.

The DNC WikiLeaks dump didn't come out of nowhere—it was advertised ahead of time. On June 12, 2016, Julian Assange appeared on British television and teased that WikiLeaks was preparing to release "upcoming leaks in relation to Hillary Clinton."[104] Two days later, on June 14, *The Washington Post* ran a story that the DNC had been hacked, immediately attributing the breach to Russian operatives.[105] Then, on July 22—just three days before the Democratic National Convention—WikiLeaks dropped nearly twenty thousand internal emails, exposing party officials scheming against Bernie Sanders.[106] And two days later, Clinton campaign manager Robby Mook went on CNN to tie the hack directly to Vladimir Putin, claiming Russia was interfering to help Donald Trump.

Russia wasn't interfering. If anything, Julian Assange was interfering. But Assange wasn't a big enough or bad enough boogeyman. Imagine Mook going on CNN and saying, "… experts are now saying that *Julian Assange* is releasing these emails for the purpose of actually helping Donald Trump." That wouldn't have served the narrative.

On October 7, 2016, *The Washington Post* released the now-infamous *Access Hollywood* tape. The recording, captured in 2005 but held in the NBC archives for years, caught Donald

Trump speaking crudely on a bus with host Billy Bush before filming a segment for the entertainment program. In the audio, Trump bragged about pursuing women and included the notorious line, "Grab 'em by the pussy."[107]

In other words, the *Access Hollywood* tape was a precision-timed October surprise—a political weapon dropped at the height of the campaign to inflict maximum political damage. The Russians didn't do that. Even Julian Assange didn't do that. An NBC staffer leaked it from the network's archives to *The Washington Post*, which published the story on October 7, 2016—just weeks before Election Day.

Worse, NBC itself had been sitting on the tape. Network lawyers had raised red flags, worried about possible contractual and legal issues if they ran it. But while NBC hesitated, someone inside the building decided the political stakes outweighed the legal risks. The tape slipped out the back door, bypassed NBC's standards, and landed *in The Washington Post's* lap.[108]

Did a single Democrat in America call this "election interference"? Did any major media outlet accuse the leaker—or *The Washington Post*—of undermining democracy? Of course not. The hypocrisy is staggering. When WikiLeaks published authentic emails exposing Democratic Party corruption, it was smeared as a Kremlin operation. But when *The Washington Post* dropped a secretly recorded tape engineered to kneecap Trump, it was hailed as journalism. The media didn't care how the tape was obtained or who leaked it, only that it hurt Trump.

Look, nobody disputes that it's painful if you're a Democrat or Hillary Clinton and real emails leak that damage your campaign. But that's no different from how it felt if you were a Republican or Donald Trump when the *Access Hollywood* tape came out weeks before the election. In both cases, damaging but authentic information became public. You can argue all day about whether it should have been leaked, but that's politics.

Where things went off the rails wasn't the leak itself. It was what the Clinton campaign did afterward. Instead of accepting the political hit, they worked with allies inside the Obama administration, the intelligence community, and the media to turn that damage into a federal investigation of Trump—based on a claim they knew wasn't true. That's the line. Leaks and even foreign hacks happen in politics. Using the machinery of government to go after your opponent is something else entirely.

But forget about the WikiLeaks release for a moment. Because in the end, it's irrelevant. The plan to vilify Donald Trump as a Russian agent didn't begin after the DNC emails leaked. It didn't begin after *The Washington Post* reported the hack. It began months earlier—long before the public ever heard the words "Russia" and "Trump" in the same sentence.

In April 2016, the Clinton campaign and the DNC hired the opposition research firm Fusion GPS through their law firm, Perkins Coie, with Marc Elias—outside counsel for both entities—acting as the intermediary. Elias formally retained Fusion GPS on their behalf to compile research on Donald Trump, work that would eventually include the Steele dossier. This arrangement was intentional. By routing the contract through a law firm, the campaign could shield Fusion's work under attorney–client privilege, treating the memos, communications, and invoices as confidential legal work. That legal shield made them far less likely to be exposed in subpoenas, later investigations, or public scrutiny. In short, the Clinton campaign wanted to hide its involvement.

Most people rightly point to Barack Obama as the central figure in the Trump–Russia narrative—the president under whose watch intelligence agencies, political operatives, and media allies converged around the idea that Donald Trump was a Kremlin asset. But Obama was not the one coordinating the expansive hoax; he remained in the Oval Office while the operation ran through Democratic super-lawyer Marc Elias.

If Obama sat at the top, Elias was the conduit through which everything flowed, the figure who managed the moving parts. Through Perkins Coie and his deep network of political and legal relationships, Elias became the consigliere—the operator who routed the funding, and concealed the operation behind the protective barrier of attorney–client privilege. That privilege didn't just conceal details; it ensured that even as every road led back through Elias, the trail could not easily be traced beyond him.

In June 2016, Fusion GPS hired former British intelligence officer Christopher Steele to produce what would become the infamous "Steele dossier." The dossier was not a single report, but a series of intelligence-style memos Steele compiled between June and December 2016. Each contained sensational and unverified allegations about Donald Trump's ties to Russia, including the notorious "golden showers" claim that appeared in Steele's very first memo, dated June 20, 2016.[109]

That initial memo, produced in just weeks, alleged that the Kremlin had been "cultivating" Trump for at least five years, that there was a "well-developed conspiracy" between his campaign and Russian leadership, and, most explosively, that Russian intelligence possessed compromising sexual material on him. The claim—that Trump had hired prostitutes at the Ritz-Carlton in Moscow in 2013 to perform lewd acts on a bed once used by Barack and Michelle Obama—would become the most infamous detail of the dossier.[110]

That first Steele memo was finished weeks before the DNC leaks were released and a full month before Crossfire Hurricane, the FBI's counterintelligence investigation to examine alleged links between Donald Trump's presidential campaign and the Russian government.[111]

In other words, the Clinton campaign's opposition research had already planted the seeds of the Trump–Russia collusion hoax, completely fabricating stories intended to tie Trump to the Kremlin. WikiLeaks wasn't the beginning of the smear campaign—it was just the excuse to take what was already on paper and begin selling it to the FBI and the press.

Let me reiterate this clearly: the first Steele dossier memo was written on June 20, 2016—more than a month before WikiLeaks released the first DNC emails. The idea that Trump was compromised by Russia was already being pushed before the emails became public and before the Clinton campaign took its biggest hit. That matters, because it shows this wasn't a reaction to WikiLeaks. The narrative was already in motion. So the obvious question is this: if the Trump–Russia narrative was already being pushed before any emails were leaked, what was it really responding to—and who was driving it in the first place?

The facts are that the Clinton plan to smear Donald Trump as a Russian asset didn't begin with Fusion's hiring. It didn't begin with Christopher Steele putting pen to paper, or even with the completion of his first lurid memo. It began even before all of that.

On March 31, 2016—months before WikiLeaks, before Fusion GPS, and before Crossfire Hurricane—the Bureau's own leadership met to discuss intelligence reports pointing directly to the Clinton campaign. Those reports, sourced from Russian intelligence and passed to the US, revealed that "the Clinton staff, with help from special services, is preparing scandalous revelations of business relations between Trump and the 'Russian mafia.'" In attendance were FBI Deputy Director Andrew McCabe and senior Justice Department officials.[112]

This was the seed of the Trump–Russia hoax. The FBI knew the Clinton plan existed long before any supposed "evidence" surfaced. They understood the political origins of the collusion narrative from the start and would eventually choose to run with it anyway.

This wasn't a coincidence. Clinton's motive was to smother the email scandal. By spring of 2016, the FBI's investigation into her secret server was closing in. The scandal had already branded her reckless and dishonest, and her campaign knew it threatened her shot at the White House.

That's why the March 31, 2016 FBI meeting matters so much. The intel on the table that day wasn't about some vague campaign tactic—it spelled out Clinton's escape hatch. A subsequent memorandum—the date still redacted in the declassified annex—spells out that "Clinton approved a plan of her policy advisor, Juliana Smith…to smear Donald Trump by magnifying the scandal tied to the intrusion."[113] She had signed off on a plan to paint Trump as a Russian asset in order to shift the spotlight off her own corruption. Trump–Russia wasn't some parallel narrative unfolding by chance. It was the cover story. The email scandal was the fire. And Clinton's plan was to smother it with smoke.

It was a bait and switch, a political sleight of hand. As the Obama administration worked with Hillary Clinton to end the FBI investigation into her, they were also working on a plan to open an investigation into Trump, calculated to keep the media and public attention busy.

The FBI's probe into Hillary Clinton, however, didn't stop at her secret server. Instead, it went from bad to worse when agents stumbled onto evidence of a pay-to-play scheme tied to the Clinton Foundation. Peter Schweizer's 2015 book *Clinton Cash* had already exposed how foreign governments and major donors funneled millions into the Foundation while Clinton was secretary of state, often in lockstep with favorable policy decisions. The book's revelations sparked multiple preliminary investigations across FBI field offices—in New York, Los Angeles, Little Rock, and Washington—into whether Clinton had effectively turned her foundation into a bribery pipeline.

But just as the evidence began to pile up, the Justice Department moved to choke it off. According to the newly declassified FBI timeline of the Clinton Foundation investigation, then–Deputy Attorney General Sally Yates issued the directive to "shut it down" sometime in March when agents pushed to pursue subpoenas, expand interviews, and dig deeper into the Foundation's finances.[114] Publicly, DOJ officials dismissed the cases as weak. Privately, Yates's order sent a clear signal: These Clinton investigations were not to go forward.

The convergence of the email scandal and the Foundation probes put Clinton in the political kill zone. It wasn't just about her reckless use of a secret server anymore; it was about potential corruption at the highest levels. That is precisely why her campaign needed a new narrative—and why the Trump–Russia hoax became the perfect diversion.

I've already told you about one glaring example of the Clinton pay-to-play scheme the FBI probe uncovered: the Uranium One scandal. But there are more examples—many more. Here's a year-by-year breakdown of the Clinton Foundation's contributions with the most reliable data available:

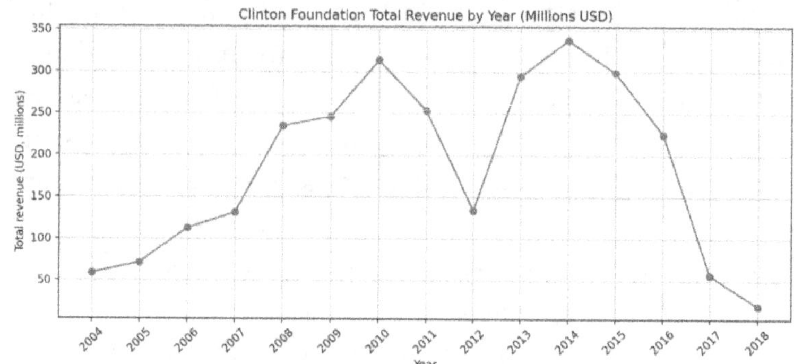

***Clinton Foundation.* Wikipedia, available at:**
https://en.wikipedia.org/wiki/Clinton_Foundation

As you can see, contributions were strong while Hillary Clinton served as secretary of state (2009–2013), surged even higher as she prepared for her presidential run, and then collapsed dramatically after her 2016 loss. This sharp decline illustrates how donations tracked closely with her political influence. The Clinton Foundation itself was established as a charitable organization whose stated mission—global health, development, and humanitarian work—did not change before, during, or after her time in office, meaning its ability to attract support should not have depended on whether Hillary Clinton held political power at all. That it did is precisely what makes the pattern look unmistakably like pay-to-play.

The drip-drip of revelations was branding her as reckless and dishonest, threatening not just her general election viability but her very nomination. Then came the rescue. In April, the

Clinton campaign, through its law firm Perkins Coie, retained Fusion GPS to begin opposition research on Trump.[115] That arrangement would soon bring former British spy Christopher Steele into the picture, and within weeks, the first salacious memo was on paper, planting the seeds of the Trump–Russia collusion hoax.

Then came one of the most brazen episodes of the entire saga. On the evening of June 27, 2016, multiple eyewitnesses at Phoenix Sky Harbor International Airport saw former President Bill Clinton stroll across the tarmac and climb aboard Attorney General Loretta Lynch's Justice Department jet. The meeting lasted roughly twenty to thirty minutes behind closed doors. It wasn't on any public schedule. It wasn't by accident. And it came just days before Hillary Clinton herself was scheduled to sit down with the FBI as part of its criminal investigation into her use of a private email server.[116]

The Clinton–Lynch tarmac meeting might have stayed buried if not for Christopher Sign, an investigative reporter at ABC15 Phoenix. On June 29, just two days later, Sign broke the story on his morning broadcast, citing confidential sources who had witnessed Clinton make the short walk across the tarmac.[117] Within hours, the "local scoop" exploded into a national scandal, with CBS, CNN, and *The New York Times* all running follow-up stories.

Behind the scenes, panic set in. Internal FBI and DOJ emails—pried loose years later through FOIA—show senior officials scrambling to draft talking points, many pages heavily redacted. Some of those emails even came from Lynch's own secret alias, "Elizabeth Carlisle," underscoring how much effort was going into keeping this under wraps. Meanwhile, FBI agents on the ground had been instructed "no photos, no pictures, no cell phones"—a clear order to make sure nobody documented the supposedly "spontaneous" meeting.

And yet, both Bill Clinton and Loretta Lynch insulted the public's intelligence by insisting the meeting was all about "grandkids" and "golf." Are you kidding me? The husband of the woman under active FBI investigation just "happened" to wander aboard the attorney general's jet, talk privately for half an hour days before his wife's FBI interview—and it was all just small talk about family vacations?

The optics were so toxic that they forced James Comey's hand. Normally, the FBI would submit its findings to the Justice Department, and the attorney general—Lynch—would make the public announcement. But the tarmac meeting had so thoroughly compromised Lynch's credibility that Comey decided to do something unprecedented: bypass his boss and take the stage himself.

On July 2, Hillary Clinton sat for her voluntary interview at FBI headquarters in Washington, DC.[118] Three days later, on July 5, 2016, Comey walked out in front of the cameras and did what no FBI director had ever done before: announce the bureau's decision not to recommend charges.[119]

Comey admitted that 110 of Clinton's emails in fifty-two separate chains contained classified information, including some marked top secret. He said Clinton and her team had been "extremely careless," that they had used unsecured personal devices overseas where hostile actors could intercept communications, and that it was "possible" her server had been compromised.[120]

Despite laying out what any ordinary American would recognize as criminal conduct, James Comey nevertheless declared there was no "clear evidence" of intent and that "no reasonable prosecutor" would bring charges—against Hillary Clinton, that is. Comey openly acknowledged that in similar circumstances, *other people* would face serious consequences. "To be clear," Comey said, "this is not to suggest that in similar circumstances, a person who engaged in this activity would face no consequences. To the contrary, those individuals are often subject to security or administrative sanctions. But that is not what we are deciding now." Translation: the rules applied to everyone else, just not to Hillary Clinton. In Comey's own words, the behavior he described would normally result in punishment—he simply decided those consequences would not apply to her.[121]

The email scandal should have ended Clinton's career. But instead of justice, she got a lifeline. On July 5, 2016, Comey gave her the "careless but not criminal" pass. That same week, her campaign's backup plan—the Russia hoax—was already in motion.

Just two weeks earlier, on June 20, 2016, Steele had delivered his first dossier memo, complete with the salacious "golden showers" tale and wild claims that Trump was in bed with the Kremlin. That was the seed of the collusion narrative.

On July 22, 2016, just days before the DNC, WikiLeaks published nearly twenty thousand internal DNC emails.[122] The leaks revealed how DNC officials had schemed to tip the primaries against Bernie Sanders, confirming what many of his supporters already suspected: The nomination was rigged for Clinton.

The fallout could have been disastrous for her campaign—but it wasn't. Why? Because the Clinton team had a ready-made diversion. Within two days, the DNC and Clinton allies declared that the hack was the work of Vladimir Putin and that the leaks were part of a Russian plot to help Trump win. Suddenly, the story wasn't about Clinton's corruption. It was about Trump being compromised.

That same month, the highest levels of US intelligence were briefed on what was really going on. According to declassified notes, CIA Director John Brennan briefed President Obama in late July 2016 about intelligence indicating Clinton herself had approved a plan to "vilify" Trump by tying him to Russia as a distraction from her email scandal.[123] In other words, Obama and the intelligence chiefs knew the collusion narrative was political from the jump.

Yet just days later, on July 31, 2016, the FBI formally launched Crossfire Hurricane, its counterintelligence investigation into the Trump campaign, supposedly based on a flimsy tip from an Australian diplomat about a barroom conversation with Trump aide George Papadopoulos.[124] But by then, the Clinton plan was already well known inside the FBI. They knew where the story came from—and they ran with it anyway.

So, step back and look at the sequence:

> June 27: Bill Clinton meets secretly with Loretta Lynch on the Phoenix tarmac.

> July 2: Hillary Clinton sits for her FBI interview.

> July 5: James Comey gives her the "careless but not criminal" exoneration.

> July 20: Steele's first dossier memo circulates.

> July 22: WikiLeaks publishes the DNC leaks, and Clinton's team blames Russia.

> Late July: Brennan briefs Obama on Clinton's plan to frame Trump.

July 31: The FBI launches Crossfire Hurricane.

One real scandal was buried; another fake scandal was born.

Was the WikiLeaks dump really the origin point of the Trump–Russia collusion narrative, or just the excuse Clinton's team had been waiting for? The evidence says the latter. By the time Julian Assange published the DNC emails on July 22, 2016, the framework to brand Trump a Kremlin puppet was already in place. Steele had filed his first memo back on June 20, seeding the "golden showers" smear. FBI leadership had already sat down on March 31 to review intelligence describing Clinton's plan to tie Trump to Russia as a diversion from her email scandal. And on July 28, just days after the DNC leak, CIA Director John Brennan personally briefed President Obama on that very plan. Three days later, on July 31, the FBI formally opened Crossfire Hurricane—kept secret from the public—while the Clinton campaign and its allies in the media began selling the narrative as if it were fact.

WikiLeaks founder Julian Assange openly admitted he wanted to hurt Clinton's chances, telling one interviewer she was his "personal fixation." On June 12, weeks before the DNC leaks were published, he even went on British television to tease upcoming leaks in relation to Hillary Clinton.

But here's the irony: Had Assange not released the hacked DNC emails, the Clinton campaign's premeditated plan to brand Trump a Russian agent might never have taken off. The machinery was already in motion months before Assange made his move. The WikiLeaks dump didn't create the collusion narrative—it simply gave Clinton's team the perfect excuse to unveil it and sell it as if it were a legitimate national security concern rather than the diversionary tactic it always was.

From that perspective, the WikiLeaks dump is a curiosity. It didn't birth the Trump–Russia hoax; it merely served as the accelerant. WikiLeaks wasn't the spark—it was fuel.

And in the end, the effect was the same. The Clinton campaign turned an embarrassing scandal into a weapon. In 2012, the lie about a YouTube video became the cover story to shield Clinton and Obama from accountability for a deadly terrorist attack. In 2016, the lie about Trump being a Russian asset became the cover story to shield Clinton from accountability over her illegal server and pay-to-play corruption.

Assange may have thought he was hurting Clinton, but in the end, he helped her more than he hurt her. By framing the leaks as politically motivated, Clinton and her media allies dismissed their damning contents as "election interference." Instead of exposing corruption, Assange handed them the perfect excuse to brand WikiLeaks—and Trump himself—as part of a Russian plot.

CHAPTER EIGHT

THE OTHER EMAIL SCANDAL

Hillary Clinton's use of a private server wasn't the only email scandal the FBI was investigating in 2015 and 2016. At the same time, agents were probing reports of Russian intrusions into political organizations' email systems, including at the DNC. The kicker is that the FBI was aware of these breaches months before the public ever heard about them. Agents had warned the DNC as early as the fall of 2015 that foreign actors were inside their network.[125] And yet, the Bureau never swooped in, never seized the servers, never treated it like the urgent counterintelligence crisis it was later portrayed to be. Importantly, all of this was happening long before anyone knew or believed that Trump would be the Republican nominee for president.

The New York Times reported on April 25, 2015 that Russian hackers had swept up "some of Obama's email correspondence" the year before. The hackers breached the White House's unclassified computer system and "got deeply into the State Department's unclassified system."[126] In other words, the hackers were able to read exchanges between the president of the United States and other officials.

Let me repeat that: a hostile foreign power—*presumed* to be the Russians—gained access to emails that President Obama had sent and received. And when the *Times* reported it on April 25, 2015, Senior White House officials had already known about the "depth of the intrusion" for months. The hacking was first discovered in October of 2014.

The *Times* noted how curious it was that the Obama administration refused to reveal its conclusions about who was responsible. Note this particularly relevant paragraph from the *Times's* report:

> But the breach of the president's emails appeared to be a major factor in the government secrecy. "All of this is very tightly held," one senior American official said, adding that the content of what had been breached was being kept secret to avoid tipping off the Russians about what had been learned from the investigation.[127]

So if US authorities revealed too much about what had been compromised, they risked tipping off the Russian hackers about how much the FBI already knew. In other words, the Bureau wasn't just protecting secrets—it was protecting its ability to monitor and outmaneuver the adversary.

There's also the strong likelihood that what the Russians obtained was so serious that the Obama administration judged disclosure itself to be a national security risk. If the breach extended into the president's own communications, as reports suggested, then Moscow wasn't just snooping on party strategy memos. They potentially had a front-row seat to the inner workings of the US government, from foreign policy deliberations to sensitive national security discussions. Faced with that reality, the Obama administration had every incentive to downplay the scope of the intrusion and reassure the public that only "unclassified" systems had been compromised—even if the truth was far more alarming.

Admitting the scope of that compromise would have signaled to Russia exactly what America suspected they knew, while simultaneously shattering public confidence in the government's ability to safeguard its highest secrets. In that light, the administration's refusal to "name and shame" wasn't simply caution—it was desperation to contain a crisis that penetrated the president's own communications.

This might partly explain the FBI's seemingly inexplicable approach with the DNC: months of quiet phone calls and warnings, but no urgent, hands-on investigation. Rather than storming in to seize servers or demand immediate access, the Bureau acted as if it were watching from a distance, careful not to spook the intruders or reveal its own hand.

Maybe.

In August 2015, long before "Russian meddling" became a household phrase, the FBI and intelligence community quietly briefed the Gang of Eight, the top leaders in Congress with access to the nation's most sensitive secrets. The classified update warned that Russian hackers had penetrated US political organizations, including the DNC.[128] It was a full year before the public would learn of the DNC hack or see a single WikiLeaks email, yet the highest levels of government already knew.

The problem was, they couldn't say so. The information they received was so sensitive that they were barred from sharing it with any other lawmakers—including the very targets of the attack—underscoring both the seriousness of the intrusion and the extraordinary secrecy surrounding it. What Americans saw as a sudden scandal in the summer of 2016 was, in reality, an operation their leaders had been warned about a year earlier, and one the FBI insisted on keeping tightly under wraps.

The DNC *should* have learned about the Russian hackers in September 2015, eight months before they went public with the information. I say "should" because that's when the DNC's IT director, Yared Tamene, received his first call from FBI Special Agent Adrian Hawkins, who warned him that the DNC's systems had been hacked by a group called the Dukes, a known Russian espionage team.[129]

The September 2015 call didn't go to senior DNC leadership. The agent didn't ask to speak with the chair, the executive director, or anyone in upper management. Instead, the warning landed with a mid-level IT staffer who had no direct line to the party's top decisionmakers—and, crucially, neither the knowledge nor security clearance to fully grasp the potential scope of the threat.

Why would the FBI alert an IT director but not the DNC leadership?

Agent Hawkins asked Tamene to "look into specific activities the FBI had noticed emanating from the DNC network that could be nefarious" and see if he could find anything to confirm their suspicions.[130]

Tamene told his supervisor, Andrew Brown, who investigated but found nothing. When asked by the House Intelligence Committee in 2017 to rank his concern at the time on a scale of

1 to 10, he answered, "Probably a four or five." Personally, if I were managing the DNC's network during a heated primary and got a cold call from the FBI warning of a Russian breach, my concern would be an eleven out of ten.[131]

In fairness to Tamene, the FBI agent's own concern seemed even lower. From September through February, Tamene and the FBI agent maintained regular contact—routine phone calls and text exchanges. Over the course of roughly five months, those continued communications seemed to carry all the urgency of asking whether Tamene had found a pair of lost five-dollar sunglasses at the pool—not whether a foreign adversary had penetrated the network of a major US political party in an election year.[132]

The FBI's prolonged, low-urgency communication with Tamene seems odd given the national security implications.

But *maybe* it wasn't odd or atypical. Tamene recalled during an interview with congressional investigators that "one of the things I should mention that the FBI had requested was that, if we do any investigation, we should do it in as stealthy a way as possible so that, in case his suspicions were proven to be true, that there were adversaries on our network, we wouldn't tip our hat to them."

While logical from a counterintelligence standpoint, it had the effect of slowing any internal response—keeping both intruders and DNC leadership alike in the dark about the FBI's suspicions.

By February 2016—five months after first warning the DNC of a possible breach—the FBI was finally ready to escalate. According to the Bureau's official account to the Senate Intelligence Committee, agents "offered the use of a cyber response team to help identify the malicious traffic on DNC's network and offered to deploy a sensor on the network." Both offers were inexplicably declined.[133]

If true—that the FBI offered assistance and the DNC declined—the only logical explanation is that the DNC did not want the FBI, which was investigating Hillary Clinton, to have access to their servers and email communications.

It's not entirely clear when DNC leadership was even first made aware of the hack. Surely someone in the DNC leadership became aware of the known but unconfirmed breach in February. Tamene wasn't in a position to unilaterally decline the FBI's offer—right?

Tamene met with the FBI agent in person for the first time in February. No DNC leadership was present—only Tamene and two subordinates in the IT department. Tamene was the "senior representative" of the DNC.[134] Was anyone in leadership aware the meeting was taking place?

Regardless, leadership was definitely aware in early April, when the FBI requested that Tamene hand over the server logs— the metadata tied to their email servers. This wasn't a casual ask. Metadata is the hidden trail every email leaves behind: time-stamps, sender and recipient addresses, routing paths, and message identifiers. In a breach, that trail can expose not only which accounts were compromised but also which specific messages were opened, copied, or stolen.[135] Investigators can cross-reference it with known email records to pinpoint, with precision, exactly what hackers touched. Even without the raw content, metadata functions like a fingerprint—mapping the scope of the intrusion, identifying its victims, and reconstructing the attackers' path. It may not reveal the words inside the emails, but it can still sketch out relationships, movements, and sensitive activities with remarkable clarity.

Tamene consulted his supervisor, Andrew Brown. In truly enlightened but uncharacteristic fashion, Brown was at last inspired to elevate the FBI's request to legal and DNC senior leadership. COO Lindsey Reynolds and a member of the DNC counsel from Perkins Coie, Graham Wilson, were both informed. That interaction led to a phone call with Michael Sussmann, another lawyer at Perkins Coie, who had previously worked as a federal prosecutor in the Justice Department's Computer Crime and Intellectual Property Section.[136]

The requested data was so substantial—"something like 15 gigs"—that it took ten days for Tamene and his team to gather and deliver the metadata to the FBI. It was turned over on April 29.[137]

But the very day before turning it over, a true miracle occurred. Around 11 a.m. on April 28, after seven months of fruitless efforts working with the FBI to detect the hackers, Tamene finally found them—except it wasn't "them." The FBI had been looking for Cozy Bear. Tamene had found Fancy Bear! Those are nicknames for two separate Russia state-linked hacking groups.[138]

DNC COO Lindsey Brown convened a conference call the next day with DNC CEO Amy Dacey; Tamene; his supervisor, Andrew Brown; and others, including DNC lawyer Michael Sussmann.[139]

That phone call led to another phone call that included Shawn Henry, the president of a private cybersecurity firm and the FBI's former top cybercrime official. At Sussmann's recommendation, the DNC hired Henry's firm, CrowdStrike, to investigate the breach, bypassing the FBI entirely.[140] According to Shawn Henry, CSO and President of CrowdStrike Services, he was contacted by the DNC on April 30, 2016.[141] This remains one of the most inconceivable developments in the entire Trump–Russia saga. The DNC, at the direction of its Perkins Coie lawyer, paid a private contractor to handle a breach the FBI had already been investigating for nearly eight months.

The DNC wouldn't have had to spend a dime if they had simply allowed the FBI to do its job. Was Sussmann's motive to line the pockets of his buddy Henry with a lucrative contract, or was it to keep federal investigators at arm's length? Either way, the breach had potential national security implications—yet the FBI just walked away. Effectively: "Okay, sounds good. We've been tracking these Russian hackers for nearly a year, but now that we have the chance to study their tactics firsthand, we'll abandon ship. Have at it, CrowdStrike!" It makes zero sense unless, of course, the point wasn't to solve the crime but to control the narrative.

CrowdStrike conducted its investigation and determined it had a "high degree of confidence" that the Russian government was behind the hacks a month and a half later. The DNC then released a statement on June 14 acknowledging the breach, using CrowdStrike's report rather than an independent FBI investigation, which attributed the attack to "two Russian espionage groups."[142] Still, the first Wikileaks dump of 20,000 DNC emails wouldn't occur until more than a month later, on July 22, 2016.

After the June 14 DNC acknowledgement of the breach, there was not even a whiff of suggestion from the DNC, the Clinton campaign, or the press that the hack was an effort by Putin to help Trump win the election, or that Trump was colluding with Putin to achieve the same end. As a matter of fact, the media emphasized that the alleged Russian government hackers had accessed "a database on opposition research against Donald

Trump."[143] That would seem to suggest that the Russians were looking for dirt on Trump.

More importantly, the media reported that in late 2014, suspected Moscow-backed hackers also cracked into the State Department and White House networks, accessing sensitive materials such as President Barack Obama's personal schedule and that the hackers had access to the information for approximately one year.

So what's the real story here? Imagine you're a journalist—not a propagandist, but a rational person. What are the obvious questions? Here's one: How the hell could the Russians gain and maintain access to State Department and White House networks for an entire year? Here's another: What exactly was the FBI doing to prevent this and protect America from foreign intrusions?

In late 2014, when suspected Russian hackers had embedded themselves in Obama's State Department and White House systems, Trump hadn't even announced he was running for president. The relevant question wasn't whether Trump was compromised by Russia. It was how compromised the Obama administration was, given that the Russians had been spying on its internal communications for over a year.

Once again, this was an Obama scandal.

After the DNC released its statement on June 14 acknowledging the breach, the overall messaging was intended to downplay the damage. This was just the Russians being Russians. "They wanted to obtain the information without it being detected. That's a kind of target that would make sense—in terms of them wanting to know things about what is going on here," Michael McFaul, who served as US ambassador to Russia from 2012–2014, told *Politico*.[144]

The very next day, a hacker calling himself Guccifer 2.0 appeared online, claiming to be a lone hacker from Romania and denying any ties to the Russian government. He accused the DNC and CrowdStrike of lying, said he had passed materials to WikiLeaks, and released a sample of stolen documents, including opposition research on Donald Trump, to prove his access.[145]

While Julian Assange teased Clinton-related leaks on British television on June 12, 2016, it was Guccifer 2.0 who first publicly released hacked DNC documents and claimed he had passed stolen material to WikiLeaks. In that sense, Guccifer—not Assange—was the first to place WikiLeaks at the center of the Democratic National Committee email scandal.

How did the DNC and Clinton campaign respond to the Guccifer 2.0 preview? Did they accuse Putin of leaking DNC documents and opposition research on Trump in an effort to help Trump beat Hillary Clinton? No. The DNC remained silent. They didn't even issue a statement. Neither did Hillary Clinton or her campaign.

It must have been a traumatic experience for the media, which was forced to report on the story and craft their own headlines without direction from Hillary Clinton and her allies. How did they cover the story?

Here are some headlines:

> *Reuters*: "'Lone hacker' claims responsibility for cyber attack on Democrats."[146]

> *Politico*: "Trump oppo book appears to show Democratic attack plan."

> CNN: "Guccifer 2.0 claims responsibility for DNC hack"

ABC: "Lone hacker claims responsibility for cyber attack on Democrats"

And my personal favorite from *Vanity Fair*: "Leaked D.N.C. Files Show Democrats Had No Idea How to Beat Trump."

Clinton had essentially clinched the Democratic nomination just one week earlier, after the June 7 California primary.[147] Trump, now the presumptive Republican nominee, was ramping up his attacks on Clinton's email scandals and hammering her credibility. And British spy Christopher Steele was busy working on his first Clinton campaign assignment—drafting the now-infamous memo about a fictitious sex scandal.

Yet for all the noise—the DNC hack reports, Guccifer's leaks, and Steele's work behind the scenes—not a single Democrat or major media outlet had yet accused Putin of trying to help Trump. That narrative hadn't launched. It was still weeks away.

But what was the FBI actually looking for at the DNC? Why did the DNC refuse to let the Bureau's agents examine their servers directly? Why did DNC lawyer Michael Sussmann—also a Clinton campaign attorney—insist that the DNC hire a private contractor, CrowdStrike, instead of cooperating with the FBI? And why did the FBI so willingly accept this arrangement, effectively outsourcing the most consequential cyber investigation of the 2016 election to a private, handpicked company?

What happened with the DNC was not just unusual—it was extraordinary. In major cyber intrusions with national security stakes, the FBI typically pushes for direct forensic access. When North Korea hacked Sony Pictures in 2014, FBI agents were inside the company's servers within days, pulling data, interviewing staff, and reconstructing the breach firsthand.[148] As the Bureau itself explained: "Sony reported this incident within hours, which is what the FBI hopes all companies will do when facing a cyber attack. Sony's quick reporting facilitated the investigators' ability to do their jobs, and ultimately to identify the source of these attacks."

When Chinese hackers hit defense contractors[149] or financial firms,[150] the FBI didn't politely ask permission—it asserted federal authority and took charge. With regard to the Equifax breach of 2017, for example, the Bureau declared: "To uncover the actors behind the Equifax theft, a broad and multinational investigative team led by the FBI's Atlanta Field Office tracked the crime's digital breadcrumbs back to the four co-conspirators."[151] Yet in 2016, the FBI did the opposite. Rather than demanding access to the DNC's servers, it deferred to the DNC's lawyers and allowed CrowdStrike to serve as gatekeeper. For the nation's premier law enforcement agency, this was not an investigation. It was an abdication.

What was the DNC hiding? And what was the FBI so eager not to see? What were they even looking for in the first place? The answers to these questions might be found in the most ironic of places—Russian intelligence memos. While the Clinton campaign and its allies in Washington would later scream about Moscow's "election interference," it was Russian reporting circulated inside the US government that first flagged Clinton's plan to frame Trump as a Kremlin asset. In other words, the very adversary they blamed for meddling may have been the one exposing the Clinton team's own meddling from the start.

CHAPTER NINE

THE RUSSIAN MEMOS

t's a fact that the DNC and FBI, through inaction, allowed the alleged Russian hackers to roam through the Democrats' servers for months unchecked. The Bureau had been warning the DNC since late 2015, yet agents never secured the servers themselves, never forced the issue, and never even examined the evidence firsthand. There's a much bigger scandal here than even "the Russians hacked the DNC and Putin wants Trump to win!"

Imagine you're the DNC and Hillary Clinton in 2016. You're under federal investigation for the private email server, with the FBI not just probing mishandling of classified information, but also circling around the Clinton Foundation. The last thing you want is federal agents digging through your communications, widening the aperture of the probe, and stumbling across material that could prove politically fatal.

Now add this: At the very same time, the FBI is investigating suspected Russian hackers who have penetrated the DNC's servers. That gives the Bureau a legitimate reason to demand access, to scrutinize logs, and potentially to expose a landmine of politically sensitive emails.

Suddenly, two separate investigations—the Clinton email scandal and the Russian intrusion—threaten to converge in one dangerous place: the DNC's own servers. From the Clinton campaign's perspective, that convergence was probably inconvenient, if not intolerable. Allowing the FBI to dig freely risked letting agents uncover not just "foreign hackers," but the kind of corruption, pay-to-play schemes, and internal maneuverings that could blow up Clinton's presidential bid before it ever got off the ground.

The FBI knew the Russians were actively spying on US political institutions, including the DNC, as early as the summer of 2015, when US intelligence officials briefed the Gang of Eight.[152] By January 2016, the Bureau had already begun receiving intercepted Russian intelligence memoranda, describing plans and operations that would soon become central to the 2016 election controversy.[153] Far from being caught off guard, senior FBI and DOJ officials were briefed on this intelligence in the first quarter of the year, months before the public ever heard about a "hack" of the Democratic Party. The series of Russian memos obtained by US agencies described Clinton's plan to deflect attention from her own email scandal by tying Trump to Russia.

So what exactly was the FBI looking for at the DNC? On paper, the explanation was simple: They needed to understand the scope of the intrusion. But by the spring of 2016, the Bureau had already intercepted those Russian intelligence reports— memos describing Clinton's plan to frame Trump as a Russian asset, even referencing private communications the Russians claimed to have seen.

That raises an intriguing possibility. When the FBI pressed the DNC for server logs and metadata, perhaps they weren't only chasing hackers. Maybe they were also trying to line up what the Russians said they had with what the DNC's systems could confirm. If so, the question becomes whether the Bureau's quiet role at the DNC was less about stopping the breach and more about quietly cross-checking intelligence already on their desks.

The January 2016 memorandum that the FBI intercepted stated, for example,

> On January 12 of this year, during a confidential discussion with Jeffrey Goldstein, a representative of the Soros Foundation on Eurasia, Democratic National Committee Chairwoman Debbie Wasserman-Schulz characterized the situation in her party in light of the growing scandal surrounding Hillary Clinton as follows:[154]

> Information released to the media in the last few days about FBI investigating possible corruption relating to Department of State (under the leadership of Clinton) preferential treatment of donors of the Clinton Foundation caused a significant negative reaction inside the party. At the same time, the leadership if the DP— [Democratic Party]—had known about the information since June of 2015. According to Wasserman-Schultz, FBI, so far, does not have persuasive evidence against Hillary Clinton because of the timely deletion of relevant data from mail servers.[155]

Let's just pause there for a moment. If you're the FBI and you're reading that—Russian intel—what is going through your mind? First off, the accuracy might shock you. It can't be dismissed because it can be easily corroborated.

The memo refers to "information released to the media in the last few days" about an FBI investigation into the Clinton Foundation. On December 13, 2015, the media exploded with coverage of newly released State Department emails that appeared to show Hillary Clinton giving preferential treatment to a family member's business interests.[156]

One widely reported example involved her son-in-law, Marc Mezvinsky, and his hedge fund's investment in a mining company called Neptune Minerals. The emails showed Clinton personally facilitating a request for Neptune to meet with government officials—an action critics saw as part of the larger "Clinton, Inc." pattern of leveraging political connections for personal and family benefit.

Do you understand how incredible this is? Do you recognize the immense irony? At the very same moment that Hillary Clinton and the Obama DOJ were scrambling to shut down the FBI investigation into her private server and foundation, the FBI and DOJ were intercepting Russian memos that were shoving the very evidence they wanted buried right back in their faces. And it didn't stop there. Those same memos weren't just resurrecting the crimes they were desperate to ignore; they were handing the Bureau evidence of an entirely new Clinton scheme to frame Trump as a Russian asset.

The January 2016 memo also makes the damning assertion that "according to Wasserman-Schultz, FBI, so far, does not have persuasive evidence against Hillary Clinton because of the timely deletion of relevant data from mail servers." If accurate, this meant senior Democrats already grasped both the seriousness of Clinton's legal exposure and the extent to which the FBI's probe had been crippled by destroyed evidence. In plain terms, it suggests her allies privately conceded what they denied in public: that Clinton faced real liability, and that her shield was not innocence, but deletion of evidence.[157]

The Russian memos were even relaying President Obama's personal role in covering up Clinton's crimes for the purposes of helping her win the 2016 presidential election. The January 2016 memo states: "Obama is not in the mood to mar the very final segment of his presidency, his legacy with a scandal around a leading nominee for the [D]emocratic Party. To deal with this he is using Attorney General Loretta Lynch to mount a pressure on FBI [Director] James Comey."[158]

The very Bureau responsible for investigating Hillary Clinton's private server and the Clinton Foundation was sitting on raw Russian reporting that explicitly described the Obama administration pressuring its own director to go easy.

The March 2016 memo summarizes that

> in relation to the consensus reached among the Democratic Party (DP) leadership regarding the candidacy of Hillary Clinton, Barack Obama sanctioned the use of all administrative levers to remove possibly negative effects from the FBI investigation of cases related to the Clinton Foundation and the email correspondence to the State department.[159]

Democrats—the very people who invented and promoted the Russia hoax—would naturally dismiss all of this because it's coming from the Russians. But there are two problems with this lazy and ignorant excuse for their inaction. First, these weren't Kremlin press releases; they were intercepted intelligence reports, internal notes of Russian operatives collecting data for Moscow, never intended for American eyes. In other words, they were candid, not propaganda.

Second, and even more important: These Russian reports have since been corroborated by American evidence and timelines. John Durham's investigation confirmed that by March 2016, FBI leadership—including Andrew McCabe—had discussed intelligence pointing to a Clinton campaign plan to smear Trump with Russia allegations.[160] Later that summer, CIA Director John Brennan briefed President Obama and other senior officials at the White House on the same plan. Brennan's own handwritten notes—declassified in October 2020 by Director of National Intelligence John Ratcliffe—recorded that Hillary Clinton had approved a proposal from one of her foreign policy advisors "to vilify Donald Trump by stirring up a scandal claiming interference by Russian security services."[161] The Russians didn't invent this story; they simply observed it happening. US intelligence records confirm their account, dismantling the claim that the Russian memos were unreliable.

The FBI's own declassified timeline shows that Deputy Attorney General Sally Yates ordered the Bureau to "shut it down" in March 2016—the very same pressure campaign the Russian memo described.[162] That's not rumor or speculation. That's hard proof that what Moscow's operatives were recording matched the reality inside Obama's DOJ.

Another memo with a redacted date explains:

> According to data from the election campaign headquarters of Hillary Clinton, obtained via the U.S. Soros Foundation, on 26 July 2016, Clinton approved a plan of her policy advisor, Juliana Smith…to smear Donald Trump by magnifying the scandal tied to the intrusion by the Russian special services in the pre-election process to benefit the Republican candidate.
>
> As envisioned by Smith, raising the theme of "Putin's support for Trump" to the level of the Olympics scandal would divert constituents attention from the investigation of Clinton's compromised electronic correspondence.[163]

The memo refers to Julianne Smith, a key foreign policy advisor to the Clinton campaign. Julianne Smith's appearance in the Russian memos is staggering when you understand who she was. She wasn't a junior campaign aide tossing out talking points—she was a seasoned national security insider who had served as deputy national security advisor to Vice President Joe Biden and before that held senior Pentagon posts on NATO and Russia policy.

Even though Julianne Smith appeared in intercepted Russian intelligence memos, she was never questioned by the FBI and never hauled before Congress. She was quietly interviewed by John Durham's team in 2021—and that was the end of it. Her name is absent from Mueller's witness materials and from any public congressional record tied to Crossfire Hurricane. For someone flagged in intelligence reporting, Smith emerged from the entire Trump-Russia affair untouched—insulated from the scrutiny that was relentlessly applied to others.

Low-level figures working for the Trump campaign like Carter Page and George Papadopoulos were grilled, surveilled, and dragged through the mud on the flimsiest of pretexts. Yet someone with deep ties to both the Obama White House and the Clinton campaign—someone specifically cited in foreign intelligence reporting in connection with the Clinton plot to frame Trump—was left completely untouched. The double standard is glaring, and the omission speaks volumes about who the FBI really wanted to investigate.

The same memo that mentions the Julianne Smith-Clinton plan goes on to explain that

> during the first stage of the campaign, due to lack of direct evidence, it was decided to disseminate the necessary information through the FBI-affiliated "attic-based" technical structures that are involved in cyber security, in particular, the Crowdstrike and ThreatConnect Companies, from where the information would then be disseminated through leading U.S. publications.[164]

In other words, the FBI never had direct, verifiable evidence that the Russians hacked the DNC. The Clinton campaign's entire plan depended on blaming the hack on the Kremlin because without a "Russian hack," there could be no Trump-Russia collusion narrative. But the Bureau, bound by evidentiary standards, couldn't simply declare it so. The solution? Outsource the job. Turn the investigation over to CrowdStrike—a private cybersecurity firm led by a former top FBI cyber official named

Shawn Henry—who could make the attribution the FBI itself was constrained from making. With that maneuver, the Clinton campaign got exactly what it needed: a Russian villain, served up not by government proof, but by a politically convenient contractor.

In light of this, the FBI's conduct at the DNC begins to make some sense. What prompted the FBI to ask the DNC for the metadata in April 2016? By then, the Bureau had intercepted Russian intelligence memos with specific references to private emails and other sensitive political communications. Wouldn't DNC metadata have been the only way to test whether those reports matched reality, cross-referencing what the Russians claimed to have with the DNC's actual records? The FBI wasn't fishing blindly; it would appear the Bureau was trying to verify Moscow's receipts.

This, of course, created an entirely new problem for the FBI. Any corroboration of the Russian memos would not only validate the need to keep digging into the DNC but also risk exposing brand-new Clinton scandals the Obama DOJ was desperate to bury. In other words, following the evidence meant walking straight into a political minefield the FBI was already under orders to avoid.

The FBI needed an off-ramp. They had walked straight into evidence that pointed back at Clinton and the Democrats. From that moment on, the mission wasn't to investigate a crime or follow the facts—it was to shield the people the evidence would have exposed. They had to look away, then justify looking away. Distance from the crime scene became the goal, not accountability.

That's more than likely why they so eagerly handed the investigation off to CrowdStrike. Not just because they couldn't definitively give the DNC and Clinton campaign the Russian hacker narrative they needed, but because they couldn't afford the political liability of being caught in the middle of Clinton's corruption. If the Bureau kept its hands on the wheel, it risked uncovering evidence that would blow open the very scandals the Obama DOJ was ordering them to bury. By outsourcing to a private contractor, the FBI could wash its hands of the mess, letting someone else manufacture the "Russian hack" story while shielding itself from the fallout of what it refused to investigate.

When the DNC servers were supposedly hacked, the Bureau had two options: conduct a real investigation or simply play along with the privately contracted sham. They chose the latter. Instead of seizing the servers and doing their own forensic analysis, the FBI handed the entire job to CrowdStrike. That way, the FBI never had to look too closely, never had to produce raw proof, never had to risk uncovering inconvenient facts that might blow up Clinton's story. In effect, the Bureau gave Clinton exactly what she needed: a veneer of legitimacy. The "Russia hack" became the perfect accelerant for her plan, transforming an embarrassing email scandal into a national security drama—and Trump into the villain.

Protecting Clinton trumped America's national security.

CHAPTER TEN

THE ULTIMATE IRONY

Both the declassified Durham annex and the declassified Horowitz appendix confirm that the FBI had intercepted Russian intelligence memoranda. The Horowitz appendix came from the December 2019 DOJ Inspector General's investigation, which examined how the FBI handled the Clinton email case and the Trump–Russia investigation.[165] The Durham annex came from Special Counsel John Durham's investigation, completed in May 2023, which was a broader criminal inquiry into the origins of the Trump–Russia probe and potential government misconduct.[166] Together, these reports make clear that the Bureau was not only aware of the Russian memos, but had catalogued and circulated them at the highest levels.

The most damning takeaway from the Russian intelligence memo revelations is that the FBI relied on raw, unverified intelligence to launch its investigation into Trump, but dismissed verifiable and more credible intelligence when it implicated Hillary Clinton. The Russian memos were intercepted communications created for the Kremlin's own use, where accuracy was essential and fabrication could cost an officer his life. By contrast, the Steele dossier was a piece of opposition research, commissioned and paid for by the Clinton campaign, built on rumor, hearsay, and politically motivated sources. Yet the FBI elevated Steele's gossip into the foundation of a counterintelligence operation against a presidential campaign while ignoring intelligence that directly implicated Clinton in orchestrating the very narrative they were chasing.

The ultimate irony of the Trump–Russia saga is that the clearest and most credible account of what really happened comes from the Russians, not the FBI, the Mueller probe, or subsequent investigations. These documents, never intended for American eyes, reveal more truth than the years of sham "investigations" conducted by US institutions that were supposedly dedicated to finding the truth. The American people were told to trust the FBI, the DOJ, and the media. Yet the most trustworthy evidence about the collusion hoax comes from the very adversary those same institutions claimed to be protecting us from.

There were two major investigations into the FBI's conduct—the Horowitz Inspector General investigation in 2019 and the Durham Special Counsel investigation in 2023. Horowitz concluded the FBI had an "authorized purpose" to open Crossfire Hurricane and claimed there was no evidence of political bias, though he documented seventeen serious errors and omissions, mostly tied to the Steele dossier.[167]

Durham went further, finding the FBI never had sufficient basis to launch the probe at all, ignored exculpatory evidence, and pursued Trump with zeal while shielding Clinton.[168] Yet both investigations quietly classified and buried the Russian memos, the very intelligence that undercut the entire collusion narrative.

It's imperative that we examine the contents of the Russian memos in light of the Administrative Mafia's desperate effort to hide them. But first, let's address their accuracy. Those implicated naturally flippantly dismiss the memos as inaccurate or unreliable. Hillary Clinton said the memos "looked like Russian disinformation to [her]." What a surprise!

When reports of the Russian memos surfaced in 2017, the same media that peddled the Russia hoax likewise moved swiftly to dismiss the contents. *The Washington Post* wrote, for example, that "according to the FBI's own assessment, the document was bad intelligence—and according to people familiar with its contents, possibly even a fake sent to confuse the bureau."[169] The problem? The CIA "assessed the information to not be the product of Russian fabrication." Nor did James Comey treat it as fabrication. He testified before Congress that the Russian intelligence was one of the reasons he decided to bypass his boss at the DOJ—Attorney General Loretta Lynch—and announce the conclusion of the Clinton email investigation himself.[170] If Comey truly believed the Russian memoranda were fabricated, then why would he cite those very reports as justification for his extraordinary break with protocol?

Now, obviously, the same FBI brass that is guilty of protecting Hillary Clinton, ignoring the Russian intel, and participating in the Clinton "plan" to vilify Trump would claim that the Russian memos were "bad intelligence." But anyone with a brain can examine the memos themselves and come to their own conclusion. And any honest person can only conclude one thing: The Russian memos are incredibly accurate.

Let's just start with the most obvious point. The FBI was aware—and by their own admission, certain—that the Russians were spying. They knew Moscow was gathering intelligence on

American politics, including Hillary Clinton's campaign. After all, they told the DNC they'd been hacked, which makes their excuse for dismissing the Russian memos all the more hollow. The Bureau couldn't simultaneously acknowledge that Russian intercepts were real and pretend that the intelligence contained in those very intercepts was too unreliable to consider.

In the March memo, the Russians reported that "the Clinton staff, with support from special services, is preparing scandalous revelations of business relations between Trump and the 'Russian Mafia.'"[171] Guess what? That is exactly what happened. Glenn Simpson, the cofounder of the opposition research firm Fusion GPS, which the Clinton campaign hired, later testified that his firm had scrutinized Trump's business dealings and uncovered links to organized crime, including Russian mafia figures who were buying Trump properties in the 1990s. Simpson also admitted that after months of research, Fusion GPS still lacked visibility into Trump's Russian ties. So in June 2016, he hired former Steele precisely because of his background running Russia operations for MI6 and his cultivated network of sources inside the country. Explaining why he turned to Steele as a subcontractor, Simpson told the Senate Judiciary Committee: "He was the lead Russianist at MI6 prior to leaving the government and an extremely well-regarded investigator, researcher, and, as I say, we're friends and share interest in Russian kleptocracy and organized crime issues. I would say that's broadly why I asked him to see what he could find out about Donald Trump's business activities in Russia."[172]

In reality, Steele's task was to produce the very "scandalous revelations" about Trump and the Russian mafia that the Russian memo had warned Clinton's team was preparing. And of course, Steele was being paid through Fusion with money from the

Clinton campaign and the DNC. The reports he churned out would become infamous as the Steele dossier, the cornerstone of the Trump–Russia collusion hoax.

What's curious about this Russian memo is that it suggests the Clinton plan was already underway well before the official story says it began. The Clinton campaign didn't formally hire Fusion GPS until April 2016[173], yet the Russian memo describing a scheme to dig up "scandalous revelations" about Trump and the Russian mafia was dated March.[174] In other words, the plan was in motion before the paperwork, pointing to a timeline of coordination that started earlier than we've been told.

In any case, the memo is frightfully accurate. It underscores that the Clinton plan was premeditated—set in motion before the public story had even begun—and it preceded the CrowdStrike "investigation," the DNC's announcement of the hack, the WikiLeaks dump, and even the FBI's official opening of Crossfire Hurricane. The sequence makes clear that the narrative of Trump–Russia collusion wasn't a response to unfolding events; it was a political operation already in the works, waiting for events to be spun into its service.

But the braintrusts at the FBI didn't even demonstrate the investigative ability of the average layperson. The same March memo states that "the political director of the Hillary Clinton staff, Amanda Renteria, regularly receives information from Attorney General Loretta Lynch on the plans and intentions of the FBI."[175] In other words, even as the Bureau brushed these memos off as unreliable, they contained detailed allegations that Lynch herself was feeding inside information about the Clinton investigation directly to the campaign.

Months later, that memo looked prophetic. In June 2016, Lynch was caught meeting privately with Bill Clinton on a Phoenix tarmac while Hillary Clinton was still under active FBI investigation. And James Comey himself later admitted that intelligence suggesting Lynch was compromised was "among the reasons" he bypassed her and announced the FBI's findings on his own.

Comey further explained that if the public learned of the intelligence in the Russian memo, "it could undermine the public's perception of the Attorney General's impartiality and the integrity of the FBI's investigation."[176] If Comey was certain the allegations in the Russian intel were nonsense, then there would have been no risk to the FBI's credibility and no justification for going rogue. His decision only makes sense if the intelligence wasn't so easily dismissed—if, in fact, he suspected there was truth to it.

Curiously, Comey offered the same justification after the infamous tarmac meeting. Testifying before the Senate Intelligence Committee in June 2017, he said the Lynch–Clinton encounter in Phoenix "capped it" for him. That meeting, Comey said, convinced him he "had to do something separately to protect the credibility of the investigation."[177]

So which was it? Did Comey take the unprecedented step of circumventing the attorney general because of the Russian intelligence suggesting Loretta Lynch was compromised? Or was it because of Lynch's secret tarmac meeting with Bill Clinton? Comey himself offered both explanations at different times.

When questioned by investigators, Lynch denied knowing Amanda Renteria. Yet she pronounced Renteria's name in proper Spanish form—*Ren-teh-REE-ah*—with an ease that suggested familiarity. Most people defaulted to the Anglicized version, stumbling over the syllables. Deputy General Counsel Trisha Anderson told investigators she was struck by Lynch's pronunciation and later told the Office of the Inspector General that she found it "a little bit weird" that the attorney general did not "affirmatively disavow the contents of the reports," according to the declassified Durham annex.[178] Taken together—the memo, the tarmac meeting, Comey's own justification, and Lynch's oddly knowing denial—there is ample circumstantial evidence that the Russian report was not some baseless fabrication, but an accurate reflection of back channels between the attorney general and Clinton's campaign.

And then there are the Benardo emails. According to the March 2016 memo in the Durham annex, Russian intelligence reported on confidential conversations between DNC Chair Debbie Wasserman Schultz and Leonard Benardo of the Open Society Foundations—the George Soros "philanthropic" network. The emails attributed to Benardo outlined how the Clinton team, "with support from special services," planned to generate "scandalous revelations" tying Trump to the Russian mafia—an operation designed to shift attention away from Clinton's email scandal.[179]

In these exchanges, Benardo allegedly explained that even without direct evidence, the narrative could be driven through "FBI-affiliated technical structures," specifically citing Crowd-Strike and ThreatConnect as the vehicles for feeding the media.[180]

Another note conveyed that "HRC [Hillary Rodham Clinton] approved [Campaign Advisor Julie's] idea about Trump and Russian hackers hampering U.S. elections. That should distract people from her own missing emails."[181]

Intelligence analysts later judged the Benardo emails "likely authentic," noting they appeared consistent with other Russian-hacked communications from US think tanks, including the Open Society Foundations. Multiple analysts noted that the Russians had hacked Benardo's emails.[182]

Even the CIA concluded the material was not the product of Russian fabrication. In other words, what the Russians intercepted was not a Russia-planted hoax—it was a window into the Clinton campaign's earliest efforts to script the Trump–Russia narrative.

But when the FBI convened a meeting on March 31, 2016, to discuss the Russian intelligence, they dismissed the memos as "raw" and unverified.[183] The problem is that every single element could have been corroborated at the time. The Bureau could have confirmed that the Clinton campaign retained Perkins Coie and Fusion GPS. They could have tracked Glenn Simpson's work digging into Trump's business ties. They could have documented Steele's hire in June to pursue the Russia angle. They could have examined Loretta Lynch's connections to Clinton—and the Phoenix tarmac meeting only underscored that concern. None of this required hindsight; it only required doing the most basic investigative work. Which means the FBI's decision not to act wasn't because the intelligence couldn't be corroborated—it was because they chose not to corroborate it. Either these were the most incompetent people in America, or they were the most corrupt. There is no third option. The record points to the latter. They knew exactly what they were doing—and they protected Clinton anyway.

Present at the meeting were senior Bureau officials, including Deputy Director Andrew McCabe, who reviewed the memo's contents with their DOJ counterparts. The very fact that such a high-level meeting was called shows that the material wasn't brushed aside as garbage. If the memos were nothing but Russian "disinformation," there would have been no need for deputy directors and senior DOJ lawyers to weigh in. Instead, the Bureau circulated the intelligence, analyzed it, and discussed its implications—only to later pretend it was never credible enough to investigate.

The March 31 meeting wasn't about investigating the Russian intelligence—it was about figuring out how to make it go away. Senior FBI and DOJ officials didn't convene to pursue the leads in the memo, but to figure out how to contain them. The goal wasn't to find the truth. It was making sure those leads went nowhere. Instead of treating the intelligence as a red flag that demanded immediate action, they treated it as a political problem to be managed, something to bury before it could threaten Clinton or expose the Bureau's double standard.

The intelligence was obviously credible, but somehow the FBI officially assessed the information to be "likely not credible."[184] Think about that. Intercepted Russian communications describing, in real time, the very operation Clinton's team was in fact carrying out were brushed aside not because they lacked substance, but because acknowledging them would have forced the Bureau to act. By stamping the memos "likely not credible," the FBI gave itself bureaucratic cover to do nothing, even as every subsequent event confirmed the reports were dead-on. Intelligence that should have set off alarms was instead treated as a nuisance, quietly filed away while the Bureau pretended not to see what was right in front of them.

The Russian memos tell us several damning things. First, they show that by March 2016 the Clinton campaign was already planning to smear Trump with "scandalous revelations" about ties to the Russian mafia—a plan that materialized almost exactly as described. Second, they report that Attorney General Loretta Lynch was keeping Clinton's political director Amanda Renteria apprised of the FBI's investigation, confirming the campaign had an insider pipeline into the DOJ. Third, the memos reference alleged emails from Leonard Benardo of the Open Society Foundations describing how the operation would be carried out. "In the absence of direct evidence," the emails suggest relying on firms like CrowdStrike and ThreatConnect to point the finger at Russia—an account the media could then repeat—while recasting the story as a domestic US issue to divert attention from Clinton's email scandal.

But the most explosive detail is that these memos were briefed directly to President Obama. He knew as early as the summer of 2016 that intelligence suggested Clinton had approved a plan to weaponize the Russia hoax against Trump. At the very same time, Obama was pressuring his Justice Department to shut down the Clinton email investigation. Rather than allow the Bureau to fully pursue the evidence against her, he signaled it was time to close the case. That decision makes him directly complicit. The memos don't just expose Clinton's scheme—they show that Obama himself was fully aware of it and chose to shield her from accountability, even as the FBI launched an unprecedented investigation into Trump on the basis of raw, unverified opposition research.

And this wasn't the first time that what looked like a Clinton scandal ended up pointing straight to Obama. We saw the same pattern in Benghazi. What initially appeared to be a failure of Hillary Clinton's State Department ultimately led back to the White House—the existence of the top-secret CIA annex, the flow of weapons to Syrian rebels as part of yet another failed Obama regime-change effort, and, most decisively, Ben Rhodes's emails. Those emails made clear the claim that Benghazi was sparked by a spontaneous protest over an internet video was a deliberate cover story, originating from the White House and Obama to mislead the public and protect him during an election year.

The Russia hoax followed a similar script. What should have remained a Clinton scandal ultimately became an Obama scandal the moment he stepped in. It required his FBI and Justice Department to shut down investigations of Clinton's email server and the Clinton Foundation—while that same FBI opened an unprecedented investigation into Trump.

Even though Clinton campaign foreign policy advisor Julie Smith claimed she did not recall proposing such a plan, she stopped short of a full denial. Smith, who was one of Hillary Clinton's top national security aides and later went on to serve in the Biden administration, admitted to the Office of the Inspector General that "it was possible that she had proposed ideas on these topics to the campaign's leadership, who may have approved those ideas."[185] That admission is striking, because the March 2016 Russian memo specifically reported that Clinton had approved Smith's idea about tying Trump to Russian hackers interfering in US elections. The campaign's own foreign policy advisor essentially confirmed the memos could have been accurate—she simply hid behind the lawyerly dodge of "I don't recall" to avoid saying so outright. In Washington, "I don't recall" is just another way of saying, *you caught me.*

It's important to recognize that the FBI and DOJ's decision *not* to investigate the Clinton "plan" or Attorney General Lynch's alleged backchannel to the campaign was made definitively on March 31, 2016. Even as new evidence emerged over the following months that would corroborate the Russian memos—Fusion GPS being hired in April, Steele brought on in June, the DNC announcing the hack in July, and the Lynch–Bill Clinton tarmac meeting—the Bureau never revisited its decision.

But the FBI formally launched its counterintelligence investigation into the Trump campaign, code-named Crossfire Hurricane, on July 31, 2016.[186] The investigation was predicated on a tip from Australian diplomat Alexander Downer, who reported a casual conversation he'd had with Trump campaign aide George Papadopoulos at a London wine bar in May 2016. Over drinks, Papadopoulos allegedly suggested that Russia might have "dirt" on Hillary Clinton.[187]

Weeks later, after WikiLeaks released the hacked DNC emails, Downer relayed this barroom chatter to Australian intelligence, which then funneled it through diplomatic channels to US officials. That's when it allegedly reached the FBI. That flimsy, secondhand account—never corroborated or tied to actual Russian intelligence—was used as the official justification for the Bureau's unprecedented investigation into a presidential campaign.

Here's how it happened.

In early 2016, Papadopoulos was working in London at the London Centre of International Law Practice (LCILP), a small, obscure think tank with curious links to Western intelligence circles. One of his colleagues there was Joseph Mifsud, the Maltese professor who operated in a gray zone between Western institutions and Russian contacts. After Papadopoulos joined the Trump campaign as a foreign policy advisor in March 2016, Mifsud cultivated a relationship with him through meetings in Rome and London.[188]

It was during these encounters that Mifsud allegedly told Papadopoulos that the Russians had "thousands of emails" that could damage Hillary Clinton. That casual claim—made by a professor working alongside Papadopoulos at the very same think tank—became the seed that, once repeated over drinks with Australian diplomat Alexander Downer, was funneled back to US officials and inflated into the official predicate for Crossfire Hurricane.

Then, on April 26, 2016, Mifsud allegedly told Papadopoulos over breakfast at a London hotel that Moscow had "dirt" on Clinton in the form of thousands of emails. By that very same date, both the DNC and the FBI were already aware that suspected Russian state actors had penetrated the DNC's servers. The DNC would hire CrowdStrike at the end of April to handle the breach privately. Meanwhile, Fusion GPS had already approached the Clinton campaign through its law firm, Perkins Coie, in March 2016, offering to continue its Trump research—work it had originally begun for another client.

The FBI briefly interviewed Mifsud in February 2017 in the lobby of his hotel while he was in the United States to speak at a conference. Mifsud denied having advance knowledge that Russia possessed emails damaging to Clinton and claimed that Papadopoulos must have misunderstood their conversation. As Andrew McCarthy observed in *National Review*, "Other than Papadopoulos's own word, there is no evidence—none—that he was told about emails by Joseph Mifsud."[189] Nor did the Mueller investigation ever conclude that Mifsud was a Russian agent. Papadopoulos himself was not interviewed by the FBI until January 2017, nine months after his conversation with Mifsud.

McCarthy makes several other astute points. Neither the Mueller Report nor Papadopoulos's plea papers claimed that Mifsud told him what Russia intended to do with any "dirt." Mifsud denied ever mentioning emails, and Mueller never suggested that denial was false. Papadopoulos later said he believed Mifsud was referring to Clinton's private server emails, not the DNC's. Those emails were already dominating headlines in spring 2016, with speculation they might have been hacked. At that point, neither Mifsud nor Papadopoulos had any reason to know about the DNC hack, which had not yet been made public.[190]

So while Alexander Downer's tip was the official lynchpin for Crossfire Hurricane, it was a flimsy one at best. Downer was hardly an objective, disinterested diplomat. When he relayed his two-month-old Kensington Wine Rooms conversation with Papadopoulos to the US embassy in London that July, after the hacked DNC emails were already public, he did so with his own political baggage. A decade earlier, in 2006, he had helped arrange a $25 million donation from Australia to the Clinton Foundation.[191]

In summary, the entire Trump–Russia "collusion" investigation that the FBI launched into the Trump campaign in the middle of a presidential election was predicated on nothing more than the uncorroborated claim of a pro-Clinton Australian diplomat. According to his account, a low-level Trump campaign advisor had supposedly told him in a London wine bar that some mysterious professor claimed the Russians had "dirt" on Clinton. He dismissed it, only to report it two months later after Wikileaks published its first trove of hacked DNC emails, none of which harmed Clinton herself. Moreover, Mifsud denied it when questioned by the FBI. That was it—thirdhand pub chatter, treated as gospel by an FBI leadership eager to justify opening Crossfire Hurricane. This shaky thread was elevated into the justification for one of the most consequential counterintelligence investigations in modern US history.

Meanwhile, the same FBI had troves of intercepted Russian intelligence suggesting that Hillary Clinton's campaign had approved a plan to smear Trump by tying him to Russia—and that Attorney General Lynch was quietly keeping Clinton in the loop on the FBI's email investigation. That intelligence was circulated at the highest levels, briefed to President Obama, and discussed by FBI leadership. Yet instead of investigating it, the Bureau dismissed it as "not credible" and moved on. Think about that: The FBI brushed aside detailed, verifiable intelligence from Russian sources, but launched Crossfire Hurricane based on nothing more than a thirdhand barroom anecdote.

In March 2016—weeks before Mifsud allegedly told Papadopoulos about Russian "dirt" on Clinton—Director of National Intelligence James Clapper quietly traveled to Australia.[192] The visit wasn't announced or widely reported, but it highlights how closely US and Australian intelligence services were already coordinating at the highest levels. That context matters, because it was Downer who later passed Papadopoulos's offhand "dirt" comment to Australian intelligence.

As Director of National Intelligence, Clapper was a central figure in shaping the Trump–Russia collusion narrative. In January 2017, he oversaw the Intelligence Community Assessment (ICA) that concluded with "high confidence" that Putin interfered in the election to help Trump—a judgment built in part on selective sourcing and heavily influenced by the discredited Steele dossier. Clapper's role was pivotal: Rather than scrutinize Clinton's conduct, Clapper put the full weight of the intelligence community behind the Russia story.

The ICA mattered because it was the US government's official narrative about the 2016 election. Released just two weeks before Trump's inauguration, it cemented in the public mind the idea that Russia had interfered specifically to help Trump. That conclusion wasn't just political spin. It became the basis for everything that followed, including media hysteria about

Trump being "Putin's puppet," congressional investigations, and eventually Robert Mueller's special counsel probe. By putting the weight of the intelligence community behind the claim, Clapper and his colleagues gave the Steele dossier and other raw, unverified material a veneer of credibility. In effect, the ICA laundered opposition research into the permanent record of US intelligence, transforming the Clinton campaign's narrative into the government's official position. And Clapper, the director of national intelligence and the chief architect of the ICA, had quietly met with Australian intelligence officials in March 2016, just weeks before Papadopoulos's now-famous remark about Russian "dirt" on Clinton became the flimsy pretext for Crossfire Hurricane.

Even if Russia had "interfered" in the 2016 presidential election with the intention of helping Trump—which the US Intelligence Community affirmed they did not know—it wouldn't change the fact that the FBI dismissed far more credible intelligence implicating Clinton while launching a sweeping investigation into Trump on the basis of a rumor.

Furthermore, the great irony is that Trump had nothing to do with any of it. He didn't collude with Putin. He didn't hack the DNC. He didn't leak the emails. He didn't hire Fusion GPS, bankroll the Steele dossier, or direct the FBI to open a counter-intelligence probe. And he certainly didn't order the media to flood the airwaves with wall-to-wall "collusion" hysteria. Every one of those actions was carried out by the Clinton campaign, the Obama administration, the FBI, and their media allies. The entire narrative that Trump was the beneficiary of "foreign interference" collapses under the weight of this reality. The only interference that actually mattered came from inside our own government—and it was aimed squarely at him.

The Russian intelligence reports came in a steady stream throughout 2016, and they told a consistent story. In March, the Russians intercepted chatter that Clinton staff, with support from outside actors, were preparing those "scandalous revelations" linking Trump to the Russian mafia. By July, another memo recorded that Clinton herself had approved a plan to vilify Trump by stirring up a Russia scandal specifically as a distraction from her email troubles. Additional memoranda followed into the fall, all reinforcing the same theme that Clinton's campaign was deliberately framing Trump with a Russia narrative.

The irony is inescapable. For years, Americans were told that Russian intelligence was synonymous with disinformation. Yet, in this case, it was the Russians who were accurately recording what was happening inside Clinton's orbit, while the FBI, the Obama administration, and the press pretended otherwise. Moscow's spies had a front-row seat to Clinton's scheme, and their reports, read in sequence, captured it in real time with remarkable consistency.

CHAPTER ELEVEN

FRAMING A PRESIDENTIAL CANDIDATE

The Netflix series *Making a Murderer* gripped millions because it showed, step by step, how the justice system could take a man who didn't fit their mold and build a case against him by twisting evidence, ignoring exculpatory facts, and feeding the public a carefully scripted narrative. The point wasn't whether the suspect, Steven Avery, was likable. The point was that the system didn't play fair. What the series revealed is that once law enforcement decides someone is guilty, the investigation no longer searches for truth—it searches for proof of the conclusion they've already reached. Evidence is bent, context is ignored, and everything that doesn't fit the story is discarded.

That's akin to what happened to Trump. From the moment he stepped onto the political stage as an outsider who threatened the establishment, the permanent bureaucracy and political elite decided he was guilty—of something. Like Avery, the case against him wasn't built from the ground up based on facts. Investigators started with the conclusion ("Trump is a Russian asset") and then went hunting for evidence to make it stick. Just as in *Making a Murderer*, exculpatory facts were ignored, contradictory evidence was buried, and a narrative was force-fed to the public. It wasn't justice, and it wasn't democracy. It was framing, pure and simple.

After Clinton campaign manager Robby Mook launched the Russia hoax on national television in late July 2016, accusing Trump of being aided by the Kremlin without a shred of proof, Donald Trump Jr. responded that Clinton would "say anything to win."[193] He was right, but what Don Jr. and others could never have realized at the time was that Clinton and her allies wouldn't just say anything; they would *do* anything, including bankrolling an opposition research firm, hiring a foreign spy, feeding fabricated intelligence to the FBI, and colluding with the press to brand Trump a Russian asset.

Mook's televised rollout wasn't a campaign talking point; it was the opening shot in a manufactured scandal designed to criminalize Trump.

The Clinton campaign's Russia plan was executed through the set of memos that became known as the "Steele dossier." These reports would become the cornerstone of the collusion narrative. The FBI cited them to justify surveillance on Trump campaign associates. Clinton's operatives leaked them to journalists, who in turn filled America's news feeds with breathless stories of treason. In the end, the dossier wasn't just opposition research—it was the scaffolding on which Trump's criminal image was built.

The Steele dossier was used to create a circular feedback loop that manufactured the illusion of evidence. The Clinton campaign and Fusion GPS hired Steele to produce memos filled with salacious claims about Trump. Those memos were then quietly shopped to both the FBI and sympathetic reporters. The media ran stories citing "unnamed officials" and "intelligence reports" that, in reality, traced straight back to Steele and his Clinton-aligned handlers. The FBI, in turn, pointed to those same media reports as validation of the dossier, presenting them to the FISA court as if they were independent corroboration. In other words, the same false information was laundered through different channels until it appeared credible. It was a closed loop of disinformation, an echo chamber designed not to find the truth, but to make a criminal out of Trump.

The first Steele memo, dated June 20, 2016, alleged that the Kremlin had been cultivating Trump for years. It claimed that Russia possessed compromising material—"kompromat"—on Trump in the form of salacious sexual activity recorded in a Moscow hotel. Another memo insisted that Trump's campaign was engaged in a "well-developed conspiracy of cooperation" with Russia to hack and leak Democratic emails.[194]

Steele's reports further alleged that Trump lawyer Michael Cohen traveled secretly to Prague to coordinate with Russian operatives; that Carter Page had struck a deal with Rosneft, Russia's state oil giant, involving a lucrative brokerage fee; and that Paul Manafort was managing the entire collusion scheme. None of this was ever corroborated. Every major claim collapsed under scrutiny.

Let's go through each allegation:

Michael Cohen in Prague: Steele alleged that Trump's personal attorney, Michael Cohen, traveled to Prague in 2016 to meet with Russian operatives and coordinate the cover-up of election interference. This was supposed to be the "smoking gun" linking Trump's inner circle to the Kremlin. But Cohen's passport showed no travel to Prague (or anywhere in the EU's Schengen Zone) during 2016. He flatly denied ever visiting. The Mueller team ultimately confirmed there was no evidence Cohen had been to Prague at all.[195]

Carter Page and Rosneft: The dossier claimed that Trump campaign advisor Carter Page met with senior Rosneft officials, including CEO Igor Sechin, and struck a secret deal to lift US sanctions on Russia in exchange for a massive brokerage fee from Rosneft's sale of a stake in the company. Sounds cinematic, but there was no evidence Page ever met with Sechin or made such a deal. The sale of Rosneft stock did occur in December 2016, but no link to Page (or Trump) was ever established. Both Page and Rosneft denied the allegation, and US investigators found nothing to corroborate it.[196]

Paul Manafort as "mastermind": The dossier portrayed Trump campaign chairman Paul Manafort as the central figure orchestrating collusion with Russia, supposedly managing a quid pro quo between Trump and the Kremlin. But that narrative unraveled. Manafort certainly had shady lobbying work in Ukraine and financial crimes unrelated to the campaign (for which he was convicted). But investigators never found evidence he coordinated with Moscow on election interference, nor that he was the architect of any "Trump–Russia" conspiracy.[197]

Despite the fact that Steele's reports were raw opposition research—funded by the Clinton campaign and never corroborated—the FBI treated them as if they were gospel truth. In October 2016, the Bureau used Steele's allegations to obtain a secret surveillance warrant on Page from the Foreign Intelligence Surveillance Court. In that application, the FBI swore under oath that Page was "an agent of a foreign power," citing Steele's claim that Page had met with top Kremlin officials and struck a secret deal involving sanctions relief and oil profits.[198]

What the FBI did not disclose to the court was just as important as what it included. Agents knew that Steele's reporting was unverified, that he was being paid by Trump's political opponents, and that one of his key "sources" had been flagged years earlier by the FBI as a suspected Russian agent. They also knew that Page had a long history of voluntarily assisting the US government in cases against Russian intelligence, something that cut directly against the idea he was a Kremlin operative. None of that exculpatory information made it into the warrant application. Instead, the Bureau elevated Steele's gossip as if it were hard intelligence.

The Inspector General later concluded that the FBI made at least seventeen "significant errors and omissions" in the Page FISA process—almost all of them in the direction of making the case against Trump look stronger than it was. In other words, rather than checking Steele's work against facts, the FBI bent the facts to fit Steele's work. The court was misled, Page was unfairly spied on, and the Steele dossier was canonized inside the government as legitimate intelligence when it never was.[199]

Even after the FBI formally cut ties with Steele in November 2016—after discovering that he had improperly leaked his work to the press—his reports never stopped flowing into the Bureau. Instead, the FBI created a backchannel. Senior DOJ official Bruce Ohr, whose wife Nellie worked for Fusion GPS, became the conduit. Steele funneled his ongoing memos through Ohr, who in turn delivered them to FBI leadership. This meant that

Steele's gossip pipeline continued unabated, even though the Bureau itself had deemed him untrustworthy enough to terminate him as a confidential source.[200]

Recall that Nellie Ohr was on Fusion GPS's payroll in 2016, working as a contractor while the firm was being funded by the Clinton campaign and the DNC to produce opposition research against Donald Trump. Under oath, she claimed she had no direct hand in contributing material to Crossfire Hurricane and that she had no knowledge of the DOJ's Trump-Russia investigation. In fact, Nellie Ohr both helped compile two dossiers and interacted directly with DOJ prosecutors. She perjured herself but the Justice Department never prosecuted her.[201]

Again, while Nellie Ohr was feeding information into Fusion GPS's opposition research machine, her husband Bruce Ohr—an associate deputy attorney general at the Justice Department—was Steele's secret backchannel to the FBI. Even after Steele was fired as a Bureau source for leaking to the media, Bruce Ohr met repeatedly with him and with Fusion co-founder Glenn Simpson, then relayed Steele's memos and Fusion's talking points to FBI officials.

This arrangement meant that opposition research funded by the Clinton campaign was being laundered through Bruce Ohr and presented to the FBI as if it came from an official government channel. Worse, Bruce Ohr failed to disclose his wife's Fusion GPS ties on ethics forms, leaving other officials in the dark about how deeply enmeshed he and his family were in the anti-Trump operation.[202] The end result was a feedback loop: Fusion GPS produced research, Steele dressed it up as intelligence, Bruce Ohr passed it into the FBI, and the Bureau used it to justify surveillance on the Trump campaign—all while the Clinton campaign quietly paid the bills.

What makes this even more damning is that the FBI already had multiple internal warnings that Steele's material was unreliable. Agents knew his claims weren't coming directly from Russian insiders, but through a long chain of sub-sources, hearsay piled on hearsay. By early 2017, they had interviewed Steele's primary sub-source, Igor Danchenko, who admitted much of the dossier was based on gossip, speculation, and barroom chatter.

The most notorious allegation in the Steele dossier—the so-called "pee pee tape" allegedly showing Trump accompanied by prostitutes in his hotel room—traced back to Danchenko, who admitted the story was nothing more than rumors he'd heard.[203]

Consequently, Special Counsel John Durham indicted Danchenko in 2021 on five counts of lying to the FBI about his sources. But when the case went to trial in 2022, a Virginia jury acquitted him on all charges.

Danchenko's acquittal wasn't vindication. He got off on a technicality. For example, one of the central charges was that he lied about a phone call with Sergei Millian, a Belarusian-American businessman with supposed ties to Trump's circle. According to Danchenko, Millian had told him about a false conspiracy between the Trump campaign and Russia. But it turned out there was no evidence, including phone records, of this call ever having taken place. Furthermore, it defied logic that Millian, a Trump supporter who Danchenko had never even met, would suddenly provide disparaging information to a complete stranger.

The defense argued not only that their client, Danchenko, never actually said he spoke to Millian—just that he *guessed* Millian might have been the caller—but also that the call may have happened on some secure mobile app, which conveniently would leave no phone record at all. Translation: it definitely happened, except there's no evidence, no record, no proof, and no way to confirm it ever existed. Totally credible! What a joke.

The whole thing collapses into farce when you stop and think about it. Danchenko didn't just "misremember" a lunch date or get a detail wrong—he *invented* a phone call with Millian, a linchpin of his Trump-Russia "collusion" evidence. And when pressed, his defense backtracked to say he *thought* he had talked to Millian. Yet that slippery hedge—"I thought"—was enough to get one charge tossed by the judge and secure acquittals on the rest. Meanwhile, the FBI and DOJ treated his shaky tale as gospel when they used it to spy on a presidential campaign.[204]

Worse still, the FBI already had reason to doubt Danchenko's credibility long before the Steele dossier became the Bureau's cornerstone. In 2009 and 2010, the FBI had opened a counterintelligence investigation into Danchenko after colleagues at the Brookings Institution reported that he was asking suspicious questions and appeared to be seeking classified information to provide to Russian intelligence officers.[205] Though the case was eventually closed without charges, the fact remained: Danchenko had been under suspicion as a potential Russian spy. Yet six years later, the same FBI relied heavily on him as Steele's "primary sub-source," treating his rumors and hearsay as if they were hard intelligence. In other words, the Bureau built its case on gossip from a man it had once investigated for espionage—a fact that makes their reliance on the dossier not just reckless, but absurd.

But it gets worse. Between March 2017 and October 2020, the FBI actually paid Danchenko as a confidential informant. The utterly corrupt Bureau rewarded him for feeding Steele the most salacious and false claims that made their way into the Steele dossier. Danchenko himself claimed responsibility for 80 percent of the raw intelligence in the Steele dossier.[206]

At the very same time the FBI was presenting Steele's reports in secret to a federal court as evidence against Carter Page, Fusion GPS was feeding those same allegations to the press. Glenn Simpson and his team of opposition researchers cultivated relationships with journalists at outlets like *Yahoo News*, *Mother Jones*, CNN, and *The Washington Post*, handing them tidbits from Steele's reports to generate headlines. In September 2016, Michael Isikoff of *Yahoo News* published a story claiming Carter Page had met with Igor Sechin in Moscow—a claim lifted directly from Steele's memos.[207] The FBI then turned around and cited that very article in its FISA application, using it as "independent corroboration" of Steele's claims, even though it originated from Steele in the first place.

This was the circular feedback loop in action. At every turn, the same raw, unverified opposition research was recycled through different channels until it looked like hard evidence. It was a self-licking ice cream cone—a process designed not to uncover the truth but to manufacture it.

In the end, Steele's allegations never held up. But because they were laundered through this cycle—Fusion GPS → Steele → media → FBI → FISA Court → media—the public was given the impression of overwhelming evidence, when in fact it was the same unverified claims being echoed again and again. This is how Trump was "made" into a criminal in the court of public opinion: not by facts, but by a deliberately constructed loop of rumor, bureaucracy, and propaganda.

Fusion GPS, the firm co-founded by Glenn Simpson, was the Clinton campaign's cutout. They hired Steele precisely because of his Russia contacts and experience. But beyond funneling his memos to the FBI, Fusion also orchestrated a media blitz. Simpson and his team met with major outlets—*The New*

York Times, The Washington Post, Yahoo News, Mother Jones, and others—to seed Steele's claims.

Through the dossier, Trump's opponents manufactured a parallel reality. On paper, Steele's memos transformed Trump from a political outsider into a Kremlin asset. The FBI's reliance on those memos gave the allegations official weight. And the media's saturation coverage, pushed by Fusion, cemented the image in the public consciousness.

It didn't matter that Steele's claims were unverified or that much of it was demonstrably false. By the time the truth emerged, the damage had been done. Trump had effectively been branded a traitor to his country. He was not investigated because of evidence—evidence was manufactured in order to investigate him. This is how a political campaign, working hand-in-glove with intelligence officials and the media, made a criminal out of an innocent man.

The methodological execution of the Russia hoax and its increasingly desperate reinventions are impressive, albeit sinister. From the Steele dossier to the Trump Tower meeting, from selective leaks to coordinated media hysteria, the operation revealed a ruthless ability to manufacture narratives on command. Every time one piece of the story collapsed under scrutiny, another was rolled out to keep the illusion alive. It was less about truth and more about momentum: a campaign of sustained accusation designed to cripple Trump politically, regardless of the facts.

On June 9, 2016, Donald Trump Jr., Jared Kushner, and Paul Manafort met with Russian lawyer Natalia Veselnitskaya at Trump Tower. The meeting was pitched and organized by British publicist Rob Goldstone, who enticed Don Jr. with the promise of "official documents and information that would incriminate Hillary Clinton." But once everyone sat down, there was no "dirt" on Clinton—only a tedious presentation about Russia's dislike of the Magnitsky Act. Trump Jr. later said it was a "waste of time," and the meeting ended without any follow-up.

A year later, the meeting was weaponized as a "smoking gun" of collusion. The Clinton campaign and its media allies painted it as proof the Trump team had sought help from the Kremlin. In reality, Mueller's investigation later admitted no illegal activity occurred. No information was exchanged, no agreement was made, and the supposed "incriminating evidence" against Clinton never materialized.[208]

Here's the kicker: Veselnitskaya wasn't just some random Russian lawyer—she was working with Fusion GPS at the very same time. Fusion, of course, was being paid by the Clinton campaign and the DNC to dig up opposition research on Trump. Just days before the Trump Tower meeting, Fusion helped Veselnitskaya draft talking points for her lobbying effort against the Magnitsky Act, which sanctioned Russian officials over human rights abuses. So, at the same time Fusion GPS was being paid by the Clinton campaign to commission the Steele dossier, Fusion was also doing contract work for Russian interests.

It was a shameless grift. Fusion was double-dipping, taking Clinton campaign money to manufacture dirt on Trump while also cashing checks from Kremlin-linked clients to push Moscow's interests in Washington. On one hand, they peddled Steele's gossip dossier to the FBI and media, insisting Trump was compromised by Russia. On the other, they were literally drafting lobbying materials for a Russian lawyer to weaken sanctions against Putin's regime. It was the political equivalent of setting a fire, then billing one client to fan the flames and another to sell the water.

In any case, the meeting went unnoticed until the summer of 2017—more than a year after it actually happened. It was only then, after congressional inquiries and investigative reporting by outlets like *The New York Times*, that the Trump Tower meeting became public. By that point, it was seized on as a retroactive "smoking gun" for collusion. Yet the fact that neither the FBI, nor the intelligence community, nor the press had raised it during the heat of the 2016 campaign underscores just how insignificant it really was at the time. It wasn't evidence of a grand conspiracy—it was an afterthought, later weaponized to fit the preexisting narrative.

The deepest irony of all is that while Democrats accused Russia of infiltrating America's democracy, it was the Obama administration that was actually spying on a presidential campaign. The FBI's FISA warrant against Carter Page wasn't a surgical tool—it gave the Bureau sweeping access to the campaign's communications. Every email, text, or call Page sent could pull in the conversations of other Trump aides. In other words, the Obama administration weaponized the most intrusive surveillance powers of the federal government not against foreign adversaries, but against its political opposition at the height of an election.

But if there is one episode that lays bare the emptiness of the Trump–Russia investigation, it is the Stefan Halper operation against George Papadopoulos.

Remember how the FBI had hung its entire case on the thinnest of reeds, Joseph Mifsud and Alexander Downer. Mifsud, the Maltese professor with long-standing ties to Western intelligence circles, had dangled the idea of "Russian dirt" on Hillary Clinton during conversations with Papadopoulos. That rumor, funneled through Downer's diplomatic report after a barroom conversation in London, became the predicate for opening Crossfire Hurricane on July 31, 2016. No evidence, no documents, no intercepts—just hearsay stacked on hearsay.

Just weeks after officially opening the investigation, the FBI dispatched Stefan Halper, a well-connected intelligence operative posing as an academic mentor. Halper's assignment was to befriend Papadopoulos, probe him, and coax him into admitting knowledge of Russian "dirt" on Clinton. To give the ruse more credibility, the FBI even sent along an undercover agent, a young woman introduced as "Azra Turk," to act as Halper's assistant and increase the pressure.

If Papadopoulos's comment to Downer was really enough to justify launching a full-blown counterintelligence investigation, then why did the FBI immediately have to send in spies and undercover operatives to try to wring something more out of him?

This wasn't corroboration—it was entrapment. The Bureau knew the foundation was weak, so it tried to manufacture proof that did not exist. The fact that Papadopoulos denied collusion again and again—on tape—makes the entire episode the most glaring evidence that the FBI never had a case.

In September 2016, Papadopoulos traveled to London to meet them. Over meals, drinks, and extended conversations, Halper and Turk pressed him on Russia. Did the campaign have connections to Moscow? Did he know anything about hacked Clinton emails? Could Trump be coordinating with the Kremlin? Time and again, Papadopoulos said no. He brushed off the idea, rejected the premise, and insisted there was no coordination. These weren't hedged or evasive answers—they were clear, categorical denials.

That should have been the end of it. If the FBI were conducting a genuine counterintelligence investigation, Papadopoulos's recorded denials would have been treated as exculpatory evidence. They would have gone back to headquarters and told leadership, "We probed, we pressured, and he denied it all—there's nothing here."

Instead, the Bureau did the opposite. Reports of the Halper meetings were written to cast Papadopoulos as suspicious, omitting the strength of his denials. When the FBI went back to the secret FISA Court to renew surveillance on Carter Page, none of these exonerating statements were disclosed. The judges were shown only the smoke and never told there was no fire.

Papadopoulos was also used as a backdoor justification to spy on Page. The FBI knew that directly asking the FISA Court to surveil Papadopoulos would look flimsy—his supposed "crime" rested only on vague chatter with Mifsud and Downer, and he had no real access to classified material. But Page, who had once been a Trump advisor, had traveled to Moscow and had a longer paper trail the Bureau could spin. So the FBI used Papadopoulos's barroom remark as the predicate to open the investigation, then pivoted to Page as the surveillance target.

The Australians told US officials that Papadopoulos had mentioned Russia might have "dirt" on Clinton. The FBI used that hearsay to justify opening Crossfire Hurricane on July 31, 2016, claiming there was a risk of foreign infiltration. But instead of seeking a FISA warrant on Papadopoulos himself, they built their application around Page—and crucially, they left out Papadopoulos's exonerating statements from the Halper operation. By hiding the fact that Papadopoulos had denied collusion when pressed, the Bureau created the illusion of a broader conspiracy, which made the Page warrant seem more plausible.

In other words, Papadopoulos was the spark, but Page was the fuel. The FBI couldn't sell the court on wiretapping Papadopoulos directly, so they used his name and circumstances to open the case and then shifted the surveillance toward Page—all while concealing that the supposed trigger had already fizzled. Papadopoulos became the pretext, the scaffolding that allowed the Bureau to spy more deeply on Trump's orbit. Without him, the entire FISA process on Page would have looked like the political fishing expedition it truly was.

This is what makes the Halper episode so damning. It wasn't hindsight; it wasn't speculation; it wasn't some mistake buried in a footnote. It was contemporaneous evidence, collected by the FBI's own informant, showing that the central figure of their case denied collusion outright. And the Bureau deliberately ignored it. By the time John Durham reviewed the record years later, the conclusion was unavoidable: Halper's work had produced no incriminating information. The FBI knew as early as September 2016 that the collusion narrative was hollow, but they pressed forward anyway.

The Clinton campaign's most desperate effort to interfere in the 2016 presidential election came just weeks before Americans went to the polls. Through attorney Michael Sussmann, their operatives pitched the FBI on an explosive allegation that the Trump Organization maintained a secret backchannel with Alfa Bank, one of Russia's largest private financial institutions. The "evidence" supposedly came from server "pings" linking Trump's company to the Kremlin.

According to Special Counsel John Durham, this wasn't just some misunderstanding—it was a manufactured narrative. Clinton campaign lawyers at Perkins Coie worked hand-in-glove with tech executive Rodney Joffe and a team of researchers who had access to vast amounts of internet data. They combed through DNS lookups, the digital "phone book" of the internet, until they found a handful of routine, meaningless pings between a Trump marketing server and Alfa Bank.[209]

Internal emails later revealed Joffe's team knew the "evidence" was flimsy and would "not withstand public scrutiny." But they weren't tasked with finding the truth—they were tasked with creating a story. So the data was cherry-picked, repackaged, and funneled through Sussmann, who on September 19, 2016, met with FBI General Counsel James Baker. Sussmann presented the claims as if he were a neutral, concerned citizen, concealing that he was working for the Clinton campaign.

The goal was twofold: spark an FBI investigation that could generate leaks and headlines, and feed friendly reporters a narrative that Trump was compromised by Russia. It worked. Just before Election Day, outlets like *Slate* and *The New York Times* ran stories hyping the supposed "backchannel," seeding the impression that Trump was under Moscow's thumb.

In reality, the pings were nothing more than spam email marketing traffic, the digital equivalent of junk mail. Independent experts and even the FBI quickly concluded the data meant nothing sinister. Yet publicly, the story was spun as a smoking gun.

On its face, the allegation was absurd. Trump could call, email, or message anyone in the world legally. Why would he need a covert communications pipeline through a Russian bank?

The answer is simple: He didn't. But the Clinton campaign didn't need facts; it needed headlines. And it got them.

The Alfa Bank hoax is emblematic of the entire Russia collusion narrative. It wasn't about uncovering the truth. It was about manufacturing a scandal—any scandal—that could be weaponized to smear Trump and sway the electorate.

Fusion GPS and Clinton-aligned operatives fed the Alfa Bank story to reporters, seeding the media with a narrative of

Trump–Russia collusion. It was a classic Clinton feedback loop in which campaign lawyers and operatives planted the allegation with law enforcement, laundered it into the press, and then cited the press coverage as if it confirmed the underlying claim. In the end, the Alfa Bank theory was debunked as a fabrication—but only after it had served its purpose of smearing Trump in the closing stretch of the campaign.

FROM CLINTON HOAX TO OBAMA COUP

n one sense, the Trump–Russia collusion hoax was the most prolific failure in modern political history. Never before had a presidential campaign gone to such extraordinary lengths to stop an opponent, and never before had such a colossal effort failed so spectacularly.

To call it a hoax is disingenuous, because it was far more than a hoax. It was election interference—plain and simple—and worse still. The Clinton campaign's effort to brand Trump as a Russian asset enlisted not only the media and the intelligence community, but the sitting president of the United States himself.

Trump's victory on November 8, 2016, was nothing short of historic—a political earthquake that stunned the entire establishment. Virtually every pollster, pundit, and insider had written him off, with outlets like *The New York Times* giving Hillary Clinton a 90 percent chance of victory on election morning and Nate Silver declaring Trump's path "nearly impossible." Washington insiders, Wall Street donors, Hollywood celebrities, and even much of the Republican elite were convinced Clinton's coronation was inevitable. Yet as results rolled in, Trump demolished the so-called "blue wall," capturing Pennsylvania for the first time since 1988, Michigan since 1988, and Wisconsin since 1984. He won Ohio by eight points, Iowa by nearly ten, and flipped counties in the industrial Midwest that hadn't voted Republican in generations. He pulled in millions of working-class voters—union households, rural Democrats, and independents—that Democrats had long taken for granted. On live television, anchors like CNN's John King and MSNBC's Rachel Maddow sat slack-jawed as the map turned red, while ABC's Martha Raddatz nearly broke into tears and CNN's Van Jones called it a "whitelash." Trump didn't just beat Clinton. Along the way, he humiliated the ruling class, defied every prediction, and proved that the American people—not the media, not the pollsters, not the political machines—still decide elections.

Still, there has never been a more elaborate, sprawling, and politically weaponized deception in modern American politics than the Trump–Russia collusion hoax. It wasn't a single lie or a dirty trick—it was an entire ecosystem of lies. It's one thing to slander a candidate on the campaign trail. This went well beyond that. The Clinton campaign and its allies planted false intelligence, federal agencies elevated it into "evidence," and the media blasted it into every living room in America.

The Trump–Russia collusion hoax should have ended the moment Trump won the presidential election. It is one thing to slander a candidate—to say anything to win—and quite another to *do* anything to win. It is one thing to weaponize the federal government against a rival during a campaign and another to continue that weaponization against a duly elected president of the United States.

What happened after Trump was elected president in November 2016 was even more egregious than what happened beforehand. Instead of accepting the results and respecting the will of the people, the very same forces that had tried to sabotage Trump as a candidate simply shifted their efforts to sabotaging him as president. The intelligence community, the FBI, and the DOJ doubled down.

The Russia hoax must be understood in two distinct phases: before the election and after the election. Before November 2016, it was designed as a political weapon—opposition research dressed up as intelligence, fed into the FBI and DOJ, and amplified by the media to damage Donald Trump and help Hillary Clinton. After Trump's victory, the hoax didn't end. It escalated and ultimately became a soft coup.

The term "soft coup" is not intended to minimize what really happened. There was nothing soft about it. It wasn't tanks in the streets or generals seizing TV stations, but it was just as insidious. It was America's own intelligence agencies, top law enforcement officials, and the political establishment working together to nullify the will of the voters. Instead of respecting an election, they weaponized investigations, surveillance, and leaks to delegitimize a sitting president. That's not "soft." That's a coup carried out with pens and subpoenas instead of rifles and bayonets.

If you take nothing else from this book, take this: Behind every step of the plan was Obama. Clinton's plan to smear Trump as a Russian asset would never have been possible without Obama's administration. The FBI that opened Crossfire Hurricane was his FBI. The CIA that massaged raw intelligence into political talking points was his CIA. The DOJ that looked the other way on Clinton's pay-for-play phony foundation and the myriad crimes related to her private server was his DOJ. Without Obama's approval—explicit or tacit—the machinery of government could not have been weaponized to launder Clinton's opposition research into "evidence" of collusion.

Presidents make decisions that shape history. That's the weight of the office. Some decisions are defensive, responding to crises, disasters, or threats. Others are bold strokes of policy, gambles meant to change the course of a nation. Lincoln issued the Emancipation Proclamation. Truman dropped the atomic bomb. Reagan challenged Gorbachev at the Berlin Wall. These are the kinds of decisions that bend the arc of history and redefine America's place in the world.

But this was different. These weren't decisions made in the best interest of the country. They were proactive decisions to deceive, to manipulate, and to weaponize the government against its own people. And both times—with Benghazi in 2012 and Russiagate in 2016—the hand at the center was the same: Barack Obama.

There are a handful of dates in American history that echo through time: July 4, 1776—the birth of the Republic. April 12, 1861—Fort Sumter, the shot that began the Civil War. December 7, 1941—Pearl Harbor, when America was thrust into world war. September 11, 2001—the day the Twin Towers fell and the world changed forever. December 9, 2016, belongs on that list, but for a darker reason. On that day, Obama ordered the intelligence community to produce the so-called Intelligence Community Assessment—the document that would claim, with "high confidence," that Putin interfered to help Trump. It was the moment election interference escalated into an attempted coup and when a campaign smear was laundered into an official intelligence product designed to delegitimize the president-elect. Unlike Pearl Harbor or 9/11, there were no bombs, no planes, no flames. The attack came from within. Obama turned the CIA, FBI, and DOJ against an incoming president, corrupting America's institutions to protect his legacy and cripple his successor. December 9 should live in infamy as the day the US government itself became the weapon—the day the Obama White House crossed the Rubicon.

I cannot emphasize enough that, at the time of the hoax, Clinton was not a government official. She was the Democratic Party's presidential nominee, but she was not the president of the United States. She had no authority over the FBI, no control over the CIA, no power to direct the Department of Justice. Her campaign could peddle smears, pay operatives, and plant stories in the press, but that's where her reach ended. The transformation of her political scheme into a weapon of the state required one thing only: Obama. Without his presidency, without his administration, without his FBI, CIA, and DOJ, the Clinton plan would have remained nothing more than a dirty campaign trick. It was Obama who turned her plot into a government operation. It was President Obama who transformed a Clinton hoax into an Obama coup. Obama ordered the ICA, not Clinton.

Normally, a report of that magnitude would draw on the full range of US intelligence agencies to ensure balance and objectivity. But after Obama's December 9 order, John Brennan hand-picked a small group of analysts from only three agencies—CIA, FBI, and NSA—to write it, instead of assigning all seventeen intelligence agencies to contribute.[210] That excluded other agencies like the Defense Intelligence Agency and State Department's Bureau of Intelligence and Research, both of which had track records of being more cautious about sweeping claims.

They produced their report on a rushed timeline and presented it as if it represented the unanimous view of the entire intelligence community. It didn't. It was a controlled product designed to tell one story: Russia interfered to help Trump win.

Brennan's role was decisive. As CIA director, he oversaw and shaped the drafting process, and his fingerprints were all over the conclusions. He insisted on the "high confidence" judgment that Russia interfered not just to meddle, but specifically to help Trump win the presidency. The NSA, under Admiral Mike Rogers, refused to go that far, issuing only a claim of "moderate confidence." That split alone proved the ICA was never a genuine consensus of the intelligence community—it was Brennan's product, framed his way and imposed on everyone else.[211]

Obama's role was equally critical. He ordered the review in the first place after Clinton had already lost, ensuring that the "Russia helped Trump" narrative didn't die with the election. By directing the intelligence chiefs to produce a report, he gave it the weight of presidential authority. When the ICA was briefed in January 2017—first to Obama, then to president-elect Trump—it created the appearance that the entire intelligence community agreed Trump was Russia's candidate.

That January 2017 Intelligence Community Assessment (ICA) was then paraded before Congress, the media, and the American people as proof that Trump's presidency was compromised. It turned the Clinton campaign's oppo research and media leaks into an "official" intelligence finding. With that stamp of authority, the collusion narrative lived on even after the election was over.

Seen clearly, this wasn't about protecting democracy. It was about overturning an election result Washington's establishment didn't like. That establishment was headed by Obama.

The January 2017 ICA was essentially Crossfire Hurricane on steroids. Crossfire Hurricane, after all, was just an FBI investigation—and it had turned up nothing. That should have been the end of the story. But instead of accepting defeat, the same forces doubled down. This time it wasn't just the FBI; it was the full weight of the US intelligence community.

By then, American agencies had already intercepted mountains of raw Russian intelligence. Yet the ICA's headline judgment—that Putin interfered "to help Trump"—rested heavily on a single, ambiguous human intelligence report. The report came from a substandard CIA source and was so flimsy that seasoned Russia analysts initially left it out of the December 20 draft of the ICA. CIA Director Brennan personally overruled them, ordering the fragment reinserted so it could serve as the foundation for the "Putin favored Trump" conclusion. A revised version was issued on December 28, 2016, and from this one vague passage, the ICA claimed Putin had "aspired to help" Trump.[212]

The fragment itself was muddled. It suggested that "Putin had made this decision [to leak DNC emails] after he had come to believe that the Democratic nominee had better odds of winning the U.S. presidential election, and that [candidate Trump], whose victory Putin was counting on, most likely would not be able to pull off a convincing victory." One veteran CIA officer admitted bluntly: "We don't know what was meant by that," adding that "five people read it five different ways." Analysts didn't know the reliability of the sub-source or how the information had even been obtained. The wording could just as easily have meant that Putin was "counting on" Trump merely surviving the Republican convention in July 2016—when party elites were still openly trying to deny him the nomination—rather than predicting Trump would beat Clinton in November.

The ICA then went even further, misquoting the underlying intelligence to claim that Putin and his circle "strongly preferred Republicans," a phrase that never appeared in the raw reporting.

Even more striking was the intelligence that was left out. Other Russian reporting circulating at the time contradicted the ICA's narrative. A longtime Putin confidant told a sensitive contact that Putin "did not care who won the election" and had often outlined the weaknesses of both Clinton and Trump. Russia, he said, was strategically placed to outmaneuver either one. Another source relayed that the Kremlin was preparing for a Clinton victory because, despite her hawkishness, "they knew where she stood and despite media stories, Russia could work with her." Still others warned that a Trump win could actually be worse for Moscow, since Republicans in Congress would block pro-Russia measures and Trump's advisors would likely take hardline positions.

Additional reports reinforced that Russia had no illusions about Trump's odds. In September 2016, the GRU warned Putin that Trump would lose the election unless "remarkable" derogatory information on Clinton was released—an intervention that never came. In fact, Putin's decision not to leak further damaging material on Clinton as the polls tightened undercuts the ICA's claim that he "never entirely abandoned hope" for her defeat.

Beyond political strategy, raw Russian reporting also detailed what Kremlin operatives believed about Clinton personally. Intercepts claimed that Democratic Party leaders worried Clinton's health was "extraordinarily alarming" and could have a "serious negative impact" on her chances. The SVR, Russia's foreign intelligence service, reported that she was suffering from "intensified psycho-emotional problems"—uncontrolled fits of anger, aggression, and sudden mood swings—and that she was on a regimen of "heavy tranquilizers." Other notes described chronic illnesses ranging from diabetes to heart disease. Still another Russian report alleged that US State Department officials were promising increased funding and political favors to certain American religious organizations in exchange for supporting Clinton abroad.[213]

Taken together, these reports painted a messy, contradictory, and complex picture of Russian perceptions of the US election. Some suggested indifference, while others pointed to a Kremlin expectation of a Clinton victory, and still others fixated on Clinton's health problems and personal vulnerabilities. In reality, a mountain of raw intelligence undermined the tidy narrative that Moscow was singularly invested in Trump's success. Yet the ICA set aside this contradictory material and elevated one ambiguous fragment to claim that Putin "aspired" to help Trump win. The result was not a balanced intelligence product, but a selective presentation crafted to fit a predetermined storyline.

The ICA was part two of the Russia hoax—a sequel to a box office bomb that no audience had asked for. Only this time, the studio doubled the budget. Crossfire Hurricane had already flopped; the FBI ran its investigation and came up empty. But instead of canceling the show, Washington greenlit a bigger sequel. They expanded the cast to include the CIA and NSA, dressed it up as an official Intelligence Community Assessment, and rolled out the marketing blitz through a compliant press. The storyline hadn't improved, but the production values had. In the end, it wasn't a blockbuster—it was just the same failed script, repackaged with more star power and louder promotion.

That selective presentation proved decisive. By January 6, 2017, the ICA's "Putin wanted Trump" judgment had been briefed to Obama, Trump, and congressional leaders, then released in declassified form. Leaks followed immediately—CNN reported on the Steele dossier, BuzzFeed published it in full—and suddenly the collusion narrative had an official government stamp. What had been opposition research and FBI speculation was now intelligence community "fact."

The same Russian intelligence that the FBI had dismissed as "likely not credible" when it implicated the Clinton campaign was later used, with "high confidence," to assert that Vladimir Putin had interfered to help Donald Trump win.

Four months later, when Trump fired James Comey, DOJ officials pointed directly to the ICA to justify keeping the Russia probe alive. Acting FBI Director Andrew McCabe and Deputy Attorney General Rod Rosenstein argued that the assessment showed Russia's interference was too serious to simply drop. Rosenstein later explained in congressional testimony: "The assessment of the intelligence community, as reflected in their public report, is that the goal of the Russians was to undermine American confidence in democracy."[214] On May 17, 2017, he appointed Robert Mueller as special counsel, explicitly to continue the Russia investigation under the shadow of the ICA.

In short, the ICA was the bridge. It took a collapsed FBI case, repackaged it as an "intelligence community consensus," and handed DOJ leadership the rationale to extend the life of the hoax. Without the ICA's "help Trump" judgment, Mueller's appointment would have been politically impossible. The sequel turned a dead investigation into years of manufactured crisis.

Behind it all stood President Obama. The ICA was not some rogue exercise in analytic overreach; it was ordered from the top. Obama had already cut his teeth on the political corruption of intelligence during Benghazi, when his White House ordered the CIA to revise its talking points a dozen times before they were released to Congress and the public. That "dry run" proved that intelligence could be massaged, edited, and laundered until it served the political needs of the administration. With Benghazi, the goal was to downplay terrorism in the middle of a reelection campaign. With Russia, the goal was to delegitimize a president-elect and keep alive a narrative that should have died the moment Hillary Clinton lost.

The ICA was the perfect vehicle. By handpicking analysts, narrowing the scope to only three agencies, and elevating one ambiguous line of HUMINT while discarding reams of contradictory Russian reporting, Obama and Brennan manufactured the appearance of unanimity. Then, when Comey was fired, the ICA provided the rationale for Rosenstein and McCabe to extend the investigation through Mueller. In both Benghazi and Russiagate, the pattern was unmistakable: intelligence bent to political ends and a president willing to corrupt the system to protect his allies and wound his opponents.

The Mueller investigation accomplished exactly what the Clinton campaign and Obama's intelligence chiefs needed it to and kneecapped Trump's presidency from day one. Though it never proved collusion, the investigation was never really about evidence—it was about paralyzing the president politically.

For nearly two years, Trump governed under the shadow of suspicion, with every move questioned through the lens of "Russia." Leaks dripped out weekly to the media, feeding headlines that kept the narrative alive regardless of the facts. Cabinet officials, advisors, and staff operated with lawyers constantly at their elbows, terrified that ordinary conversations could be twisted into "obstruction." Foreign leaders and domestic allies alike saw Trump as weakened, unsure whether he would survive politically or even legally.

Key policy priorities stalled. Any attempt by Trump to challenge the intelligence community, reform the FBI, or reset relations with Russia was instantly branded as proof he was "compromised." Every social media post, firing, or private conversation was treated as a potential "smoking gun." In this way, Mueller's probe boxed Trump into a defensive crouch. The president of the United States spent his first two years consumed with fighting an allegation that was fabricated from the start.

By the time Mueller finally admitted in 2019 that there was no evidence of collusion, the damage was already done. Trump's presidency had been hobbled, his agenda delayed, and his credibility permanently scarred. The investigation's true legacy wasn't justice or truth—it was the successful use of a manufactured hoax to cripple an elected president.

The Mueller investigation also shielded Obama and Clinton from scrutiny. While every headline, hearing, and leak revolved around the phantom of "Trump–Russia collusion," there was no parallel investigation into how the hoax itself began. The Clinton campaign's role in bankrolling the Steele dossier was buried. Fusion GPS's coordination with Democratic lawyers and friendly reporters was ignored. The FBI's reliance on raw opposition research for FISA warrants never made the evening news.

Most importantly, Obama's own role in ordering the ICA and shaping the Russia narrative was placed beyond reach. By framing Trump as the subject under suspicion, the Mueller probe flipped the script. The investigators became untouchable, and the architects of the hoax—Obama, Brennan, Comey, and Clinton—enjoyed de facto immunity. Scandals that should have been investigated—Clinton's private email server, the Benghazi cover-up, the pay-to-play deals at the Clinton Foundation, and even the weaponization of intelligence in 2016—were all pushed off the table.

In this way, Mueller's probe was a two-edged sword. It paralyzed Trump while protecting those who had conspired against him. Instead of exposing corruption, the investigation became a shield for it—ensuring that the perpetrators of the hoax never faced accountability.

If there was ever a nonpartisan, unifying problem that truly demanded attention, it wasn't the hoax of Trump–Russia collusion—it was the genuine evidence of Russian infiltration. The raw intelligence showed just how effectively Russian intelligence services had penetrated US political institutions and gained visibility into the inner workings of the American government. Moscow was receiving detailed reports on campaign strategies, backchannel communications, even private assessments of Hillary Clinton's health. The Russians had a front-row seat to American politics at its highest levels.

That should have been the story. That should have prompted a bipartisan reckoning about the vulnerabilities of America's political system and the failure of our intelligence agencies to detect and prevent it. Instead, that raw intelligence was dismissed, buried, or twisted into political ammunition. The very evidence of Russian penetration that could have united Americans in a common effort to protect the republic was ignored because it contradicted the narrative that Clinton and Obama needed.

By focusing on a fabricated "collusion" scandal, Washington not only kneecapped Trump—it kneecapped America's ability to confront the real problem. The raw intelligence showed that Russian services had successfully infiltrated and monitored the US political class, yet those vulnerabilities were left unexamined and unaddressed. The hoax diverted attention away from genuine threats, leaving the nation weaker, not stronger, in the face of foreign espionage.

The Mueller investigation turned into a broad witch hunt that poisoned American politics. It didn't uncover collusion, but it did succeed in dragging dozens of people into years of legal jeopardy—not for conspiring with Russia, but for process crimes, financial missteps, or unrelated matters dredged up along the way. Trump aides were bankrupted by legal fees, families were ruined, and reputations were destroyed, all while the headlines screamed "Russia, Russia, Russia." The real legacy of the probe wasn't justice, but division. It entrenched mistrust in government, deepened partisan bitterness, and convinced millions of Americans that Washington's institutions could be weaponized to crush political opponents.

George Papadopoulos was a twenty-eight-year-old, low-level foreign policy aide on the Trump campaign. His "crime" wasn't collusion with Russia, but misstating the timing of his contacts with a professor who boasted about Moscow having "dirt" on Hillary Clinton. He told the FBI in January 2017 that Joseph Mifsud had spoken to him before he joined the Trump campaign, when in fact it was shortly after. The FBI already knew the real timeline, so nothing was concealed. Still, Mueller's team turned this trivial slip into a felony, parading it as proof of "collusion" when it showed the case's emptiness.

For that slip, Mueller's team charged him with lying to the FBI. Papadopoulos pled guilty, served twelve days in prison, and was saddled with a felony record. His case was spun in the press as the "spark" of Russiagate, when in reality it showed how little there was to the entire narrative.

Michael Flynn, Trump's first national security advisor and a decorated three-star general, was accused of lying to the FBI about conversations with the Russian ambassador—conversations that were entirely normal for an incoming national security chief. FBI agents themselves initially said Flynn hadn't lied, but the bureau pressed on anyway. After being bankrupted by legal fees, Flynn pled guilty under pressure. Years later, the DOJ admitted the case was tainted, and Trump pardoned him. Flynn's ordeal symbolized how the investigation was weaponized to destroy reputations.

Paul Manafort and Rick Gates, Trump's former campaign chairman and his deputy respectively, weren't charged with collusion at all. Instead, Mueller dug into their old consulting work for Ukrainian clients years before the 2016 campaign. Manafort was convicted of tax and bank fraud and sentenced to 7.5 years, later pardoned. Gates pled guilty and received a reduced sentence after cooperating. These prosecutions made headlines but had nothing to do with Trump–Russia collusion.

Roger Stone, a longtime Trump ally, was targeted for alleged lies to Congress about his contacts with WikiLeaks. He was convicted of obstruction, lying, and witness tampering—all process crimes. In a heavy-handed move, Mueller's prosecutors even sent a tactical team to raid his home in a pre-dawn, televised spectacle. Stone's sentence was later commuted and pardoned. His case epitomized the theatrical, punitive nature of the investigation.

Michael Cohen, Trump's personal lawyer, wasn't even prosecuted by Mueller directly, but only through referrals. He pled guilty to campaign finance violations and tax charges, serving three years in prison. His downfall was splashed across the headlines as proof of "Trump world corruption," yet it had nothing whatsoever to do with Russian collusion.

Alex van der Zwaan, a Dutch attorney with peripheral ties to Manafort and Gates, was charged for lying to investigators.

His punishment? Thirty days in prison. His case made clear that Mueller's team was determined to notch as many "scalps" as possible, no matter how minor.

Every prominent American caught up in the Mueller dragnet was charged with process crimes, old business dealings, or unrelated offenses, not collusion with Russia. Yet the spectacle of raids, indictments, and guilty pleas created the illusion that Mueller had uncovered a massive conspiracy. In reality, it was a broad witch hunt that ruined lives, dominated headlines, and soured American politics, all while the central allegation of Trump–Russia collusion collapsed.

The Mueller probe ushered in a new era of prosecutorial misconduct where the government no longer investigated crimes to find culprits, but investigated people in search of crimes. It was the inversion of American justice, echoing Lavrentiy Beria's infamous boast under Stalin: "Show me the man, and I'll show you the crime." In practice, this meant targeting Trump's allies not for collusion with Russia, but for paperwork errors, misremembered conversations, or unrelated business dealings dredged up years later. It was a modern form of political persecution cloaked in the authority of law, and it left a chilling message: If the government sets its sights on you, it will find something to charge you with.

General Flynn's case was particularly egregious because it revealed just how far the FBI was willing to bend the rules to entrap a political target. As Trump's incoming national security advisor, Flynn had routine conversations with Russian ambassador Sergey Kislyak during the transition—the kind of calls any national security appointee would make.

The FBI already had a verbatim transcript of Flynn's December 29, 2016 call through routine surveillance of Kislyak.

Yet on January 24, 2017, agents Peter Strzok and Joe Pientka went to the White House without notifying the White House Counsel, deliberately catching Flynn off guard. They told him he didn't need a lawyer and framed the meeting as a "casual conversation."

When Flynn said he had not asked Kislyak to refrain from escalating sanctions and claimed they hadn't discussed expulsions, the Bureau compared his recollections against their transcript. Those minor discrepancies became the basis for charging him with making false statements.

Flynn didn't even directly tell Kislyak "not to escalate." He said Russia should "respond in a measured way" and "avoid escalating the situation." In other words, the very phrasing the FBI used to accuse him of lying wasn't in the transcript at all. It was an interpretation—one the Bureau twisted into a felony charge.[215]

Declassified FBI notes exposed the true intent: "What's our goal? Truth/admission or to get him to lie, so we can prosecute him or get him fired?"[216] It was a perjury trap, plain and simple. Comey later bragged about exploiting the Trump team's inexperience, admitting in 2018: "I sent them. Something I probably wouldn't have gotten away with in a more…organized administration."[217] Flynn's ordeal, during which he was coerced into pleading guilty under threat that prosecutors would target his son, epitomized how the Russia hoax twisted justice not to uncover crimes, but to manufacture them.

Flynn eventually pled guilty under crushing financial and legal pressure. He later sought to withdraw his plea, citing FBI misconduct after evidence surfaced that agents had debated whether their "goal" was to get him to lie so they could prosecute him.

In May 2020, the Justice Department admitted Flynn should never have been prosecuted and moved to dismiss the case, acknowledging that his statements were not "material" to any legitimate investigation. Yet Judge Emmet Sullivan refused to grant dismissal, instead appointing an outside former judge to argue against the DOJ's own motion. Even when the government confessed its wrongdoing, the court still wouldn't let Flynn go.

His struggles only ended when President Trump issued a full pardon in November 2020. The Flynn case epitomized the misconduct of the Mueller era. A decorated general was destroyed not for collusion with Russia, but because the FBI saw him as a convenient pawn in its campaign to kneecap Trump.

Flynn's downfall didn't happen in a vacuum. It was set up by President Obama himself in his final weeks in office. On December 29, 2016, Obama abruptly escalated tensions with Russia by expelling thirty-five diplomats and closing two compounds—a dramatic move announced just three weeks before Trump was to take office.[218] This last-minute action was less about foreign policy than it was about laying a trap. It created a volatile situation that would inevitably require Trump's incoming national security team to engage with Moscow to keep things from spiraling. That engagement, in turn, gave the FBI the perfect pretext to target Flynn.

Compare that to Igor Danchenko, Steele's primary source for his infamous dossier of bullshit, who told the FBI that Sergei Millian had personally fed him information about Trump's ties to Russia. Danchenko claimed he had received a phone call from an anonymous person he "believed" was Millian. Phone records proved the call never happened, but the defense floated the possibility it could have been made through an app not captured by phone records. He walked free on that technicality.

And Peter Strzok, the FBI agent who helped launch Crossfire Hurricane, interviewed Flynn, and texted his own mistress that "we'll stop" Trump—was never prosecuted at all.

Strzok's mistress, Lisa Page, was not some outsider—she was an FBI lawyer who served as special counsel to Deputy Director Andrew McCabe and worked directly with Strzok on both the Clinton email investigation and Crossfire Hurricane. The two carried on an affair while exchanging text messages that revealed stunning political bias, including Page asking if Trump would ever become president and Strzok replying, "No. No he's not. We'll stop it."[219] Both eventually left the Bureau—Page resigned in 2018, and Strzok was fired the same year—yet neither faced prosecution. Instead, they reinvented themselves as anti-Trump media figures, with Page landing a legal analyst role at NBC/ MSNBC and Strzok publishing a book and suing the DOJ for wrongful termination. The irony is glaring: While Trump's allies were destroyed over trivial process charges, the FBI insiders who rigged the game against them walked away unpunished, even profiting from their misconduct.

Leaking classified information is a federal crime under the Espionage Act. Comey admitted leaking his FBI memos—several of which contained classified information—through an intermediary to the press. The DOJ inspector general concluded that he violated FBI policy and mishandled official records, yet prosecutors declined to charge him. For ordinary agents or military personnel, this same act has resulted in felony convictions and prison sentences. Comey's escape from accountability exposed a blatant double standard: What is a clear violation of the Espionage Act for everyone else was excused for the former FBI director.

In 2017, no Democrat worked harder than Adam Schiff to convince the American public that Donald Trump was guilty of collusion with Russia, and no one lied more brazenly in the process. Over and over again, Schiff went on television and claimed he had personally seen "more than circumstantial evidence" of collusion, suggesting there was direct proof that Trump and his campaign were conspiring with the Kremlin.

He told ABC that the evidence was "as clear as you could find," and he told CNN that the chain of events was "pretty damning." Yet when the investigations finally concluded—Mueller, the DOJ, and even bipartisan Senate reports—none had found the collusion Schiff promised existed. The "evidence" Schiff insisted he had seen simply did not exist. His repeated appearances, presented with the gravitas of an insider who had access to classified intelligence, were not misstatements or exaggerations. They were deliberate lies, calculated to poison public opinion against a sitting president and to keep alive the illusion of a scandal that was collapsing under its own weight.

Adam Schiff, once the face of Trump–Russia allegations in the House, has since been elevated to the US Senate. Now, barely into his new role, he finds himself under federal investigation for alleged mortgage fraud. Prosecutors are examining whether Schiff falsely claimed both his Maryland and California properties as "primary residences" to secure below-market interest rates and tax breaks, potentially saving tens of thousands of dollars.[220] The Department of Justice is weighing charges of bank, mail, and wire fraud—serious felonies that carry heavy prison terms—yet Schiff insists he has done nothing wrong and portrays the probe as political retaliation. The irony is striking: the man who once championed investigations into others now stands as a senator under investigation himself.

Michael Sussmann, the Clinton campaign lawyer who peddled the false Alfa Bank "Trump–Russia backchannel" hoax, was charged by Special Counsel John Durham with lying to the FBI. Billing records, texts, and testimony showed he told the Bureau he wasn't representing any client, when in fact he was working for Hillary Clinton's campaign and a tech executive who provided him with the white papers.

In any honest system, that's a clear violation of the federal false-statements statute. Yet in Washington, DC, where juries are overwhelmingly partisan, Sussmann walked free. The same Department of Justice that looked the other way when a Clinton ally misled the FBI has zealously prosecuted Trump associates like Michael Flynn, Steve Bannon, and Peter Navarro for far less. It's one set of rules for Democrats, another for anyone tied to Donald Trump.

Hillary Clinton's campaign, working through its law firm Perkins Coie, deliberately concealed its funding of the Steele dossier by routing payments as "legal services" rather than opposition research. In reality, those millions of dollars were funneled to Fusion GPS, which then hired Christopher Steele to produce the discredited Trump–Russia dossier. By disguising the expense in official filings with the Federal Election Commission (FEC), the campaign avoided disclosing the true nature of its spending. The FEC later fined both the Clinton campaign and the DNC for this misreporting, underscoring that the concealment was not a mere clerical error, but a violation of campaign finance law designed to hide the origins of a political weapon.

While Hillary Clinton's 2016 campaign was fined by the FEC for disguising payments to Fusion GPS as "legal services" rather than opposition research, no one faced criminal charges.

By contrast, in March 2023, Manhattan District Attorney Alvin Bragg indicted Trump over the 2016 payment to Stormy Daniels, claiming it was an unreported campaign expense.[221] In May 2024, a New York jury convicted Trump on thirty-four felony counts tied to this so-called "hush money" case, with sentencing scheduled later that year. Clinton's concealment of millions in opposition research was brushed off with a fine, while Trump's handling of a personal nondisclosure agreement was elevated into felony convictions carrying the threat of prison.

The Trump–Russia collusion saga stands as one of the most destructive political hoaxes in modern American history. Born out of opposition research secretly financed by Hillary Clinton's campaign, it was laundered through law firms, intelligence operatives, and a compliant press until it appeared to be legitimate intelligence.

What followed was years of FBI surveillance, a special counsel investigation, congressional hearings, and nonstop media hysteria, all on the back of unverified claims that never held up under scrutiny. It was not only an attack on Donald Trump, but an assault on the integrity of American democracy itself.

As previously mentioned, there have been two investigations into the origins of the Trump–Russia affair—one led by DOJ Inspector General Michael Horowitz and the other by Special Counsel John Durham. Horowitz's reports laid bare the FBI's misconduct, including doctored evidence in the FISA process, but as an internal watchdog, he had no power to indict.

Durham, by contrast, had prosecutorial authority and did bring charges. Three men were indicted: FBI lawyer Kevin Clinesmith, who pled guilty to falsifying an email in the Carter Page warrant and received probation; Clinton campaign lawyer Michael Sussmann, who was acquitted after lying to the FBI about his Alfa Bank tip; and dossier source Igor Danchenko, who was also acquitted of lying to investigators. In the end, only Clinesmith was convicted, and he avoided prison.

Clinesmith was an FBI lawyer working on the Page FISA warrants, and he committed outright fraud to keep the surveillance alive. In 2017, the CIA told the FBI that Page had actually been an "operational contact" who had assisted US intelligence in the past. That should have undercut the FBI's entire case because if Page had helped the CIA, he wasn't a Russian agent. Instead of reporting that truth, Clinesmith altered a CIA email to say the exact opposite: that Page was "not a source."[222]

Page was portrayed by the FBI as a suspicious Trump advisor secretly working with Russia. But the truth was that Page had been an informant for the CIA, providing information about his contacts with Russians to US intelligence for years. That history would have completely changed the picture. Instead of looking like a Russian agent, Page looked like a loyal American who had already been helping his own government.

That's why Clinesmith's falsification mattered so much. By altering the CIA's email to say Page was *not* a source, the FBI erased the most important piece of context. Page wasn't hiding Russian ties; he was reporting them. Had the FISA Court known this, it would have undermined the entire basis for surveillance. The FBI would have lost its justification for spying not just on Page but on the Trump campaign itself, since Page's warrant gave investigators access to campaign communications.

In short, Clinesmith's deception covered up exculpatory evidence, flipped the truth on its head, and allowed the FBI to continue surveillance it otherwise couldn't have lawfully justified. It was a small lie with massive consequences, since without it, the wiretap likely would have collapsed.

The story of Crossfire Hurricane was never about protecting America from foreign threats; it was about protecting the political establishment from Trump. From the moment Hillary Clinton's campaign seeded the collusion narrative, the FBI, DOJ, and intelligence community bent every rule to keep it alive. They tried to entrap George Papadopoulos, hid exculpatory evidence from the courts, and even falsified documents to sustain illegal surveillance of Page. And when their misconduct was exposed, the system responded not with accountability, but with shrugs and wrist slaps.

This is the enduring legacy of the Trump–Russia collusion hoax. What began as a smear through opposition research became a federal investigation, then a special counsel probe, then years of headlines, all designed to weaken a duly elected president. That is why the Trump–Russia affair was an attempted coup, executed not with tanks in the streets but with leaks, lies, and lawfare. The real danger was never Moscow meddling in our elections—it was our own institutions conspiring to overthrow the will of the people. And in that sense, the collusion hoax did lasting damage. It taught a generation of Americans that those entrusted with justice are willing to corrupt it when power is at stake.

CHAPTER THIRTEEN

THE FISH ROTS FROM THE HEAD

You never would have had the Trump–Russia collusion hoax without Benghazi, because Benghazi is what exposed Hillary Clinton's private email server and, by extension, the Clinton Foundation's conflicts of interest. But the reason it got that far traces back to Barack Obama's decision on September 11, 2012, to blame the attack on a "spontaneous protest" over a YouTube video rather than admit it was a premeditated act of terrorism. That political cover-up forced investigations, which uncovered Clinton's secret server, which in turn revealed her reckless handling of classified information and her ties to Clinton Foundation donors. By 2016, Clinton's campaign was drowning in scandal and needed a counter-narrative dramatic enough to bury her own misconduct. The Russia hoax was that narrative.

Barack Obama was permitted to get away with everything. Shielded by the historic nature of his presidency, by his race, and by a fawning media, he faced almost no scrutiny for scandals that would have destroyed anyone else. The fish rots from the head, and under Obama, the rot spread unchecked. For him and his allies, it bred an intoxicating sense of invincibility. But the rule of cover-ups is simple: The bigger the crime, the bigger the lie required to conceal it. That's why the Trump–Russia collusion hoax had to be so massive in scale. Because what it was designed to obscure—the failures, corruption, and lawlessness of the Obama–Clinton years—was itself massive and unprecedented.

Trump–Russia collusion didn't just "happen." It was carried out by career criminals masquerading as politicians, prosecutors, and bureaucrats—and the cast of characters tells the story. Adam Schiff, the hoax's loudest salesman, pushed false claims of "secret evidence" against Trump while his own name was tied to a mortgage fraud scandal back in California. Letitia James, who campaigned for Attorney General on the promise to "get Trump," has also faced scrutiny for her own shady involvement in mortgage fraud schemes.[223] James Comey, who weaponized the FBI, walked away with a million-dollar book deal and a speaking tour. Andrew McCabe, caught lying under oath, was rewarded with a CNN contract. John Brennan, who bent intelligence to fit Obama's needs, landed a permanent seat on MSNBC. John Bolton, entrusted with America's secrets, turned around and monetized classified information in a tell-all book. Hillary Clinton funneled donor money through the Clinton Foundation while laundering opposition research into official FBI investigations. This ecosystem doesn't punish corruption; it rewards it. In Washington's Administrative Mafia, liars, leakers, and lawbreakers are promoted and protected—and the Trump–Russia hoax was their crowning achievement.

This was an unprecedented crime against America and the American citizenry. For the first time, the full weight of the nation's intelligence and law enforcement apparatus was weaponized to undermine a presidential candidate and, later, a sitting president. The damage was not temporary, nor was it confined to one election cycle. It tore at the fabric of trust between the governed and those who govern. It proved that unelected bureaucrats and political operatives were willing to weaponize the state to nullify an election. The long-held tradition of the peaceful transfer of power—the bedrock of our republic—was broken, and with it, the innocence of American democracy.

Modern American history can now be divided in two: before the Russia hoax and after.

At its core, the Trump–Russia collusion hoax involved a web of serious crimes. It began with the Clinton campaign secretly funding fabricated opposition research and laundering it through law firms and cut-outs—a classic case of campaign finance fraud and conspiracy to defraud the United States. That bogus material was then fed into the FBI, which used it to obtain FISA warrants under false pretenses, resulting in unlawful spying on American citizens, including Trump campaign advisor Carter Page.

Along the way, FBI officials doctored documents, withheld exculpatory evidence, and misled the secret FISA court, amounting to perjury and obstruction of justice. Operatives like Michael Sussmann lied about who they were representing when meeting with the FBI, which is a felony under the false-statements statute. Then, with the help of a compliant media, classified leaks were strategically dripped to the press—criminal mishandling of classified information—to keep the fake narrative alive. Taken together, this was not politics as usual; it was a sprawling criminal enterprise that abused America's law enforcement and intelligence powers to frame a political opponent.

This was the very abusive behavior that the Founding Fathers cited as justification to declare their independence. In 1776, Jefferson warned that "when a long train of abuses and usurpations, pursuing invariably the same Object evinces a design to reduce them under absolute Despotism, it is their right, it is their duty, to throw off such Government." What America witnessed in 2016 was the modern echo of that warning and the culmination of all their fears.

The United States Constitution is unique in all the world because it establishes a relationship between the government and the governed unlike any other. Power flows upward, not downward; authority is derived from the consent of the people, not bestowed upon them by rulers. For over two centuries, this principle safeguarded the republic. Leaders came and went, parties rose and fell, but the people's choice was honored, and the peaceful transfer of power endured.

The Russia hoax severed that sacred covenant. It was not merely a scandal; it was an assault on the very framework that makes America exceptional—the United States is the world's longest-running continuous constitutional democracy. For more than two centuries, power has changed hands not by revolution or decree, but by the will of the voters expressed at the ballot box. Before 2016, Americans could believe that even bitter political disputes would ultimately be decided by voters. After 2016, that faith was broken. History will remember it as the moment the ruling class showed its willingness to override the will of the people—and the moment the people were reminded that liberty survives only so long as they are willing to defend it.

No one responsible for carrying out the greatest crime against the American people and our republic has been held accountable. The architects of the Russia hoax—from political operatives who manufactured the lies, to FBI officials who bent the law, to intelligence chiefs who concealed the truth, and even the president who approved the coup—have all walked away virtually unscathed.

Every sprawling conspiracy has a point of origin, a keystone figure without whom the entire structure collapses. In the Trump–Russia collusion hoax, that man remains Marc Elias. He was not a household name like Hillary Clinton, James Comey, or John Brennan. He preferred to operate in the shadows, always ready to invoke "attorney–client privilege" and silence anyone who drifted too close to the truth. But make no mistake: Elias was the lynchpin, the indispensable man, the keystone without whom the coup never would have stood.

As Hillary Clinton's campaign counsel, it was Elias who hired Fusion GPS. It was Elias who approved the payments that funded Steele and his now-discredited dossier. It was Elias who engineered the legal firewall that allowed opposition research to masquerade as intelligence, funneled through the FBI and into the bloodstream of government investigations. Without him, there would have been no Steele dossier, no FISA warrants on Trump associates, and no justification for Crossfire Hurricane. In many ways his role was the most elusive but significant of all.

His fingerprints don't stop there. In deposition after deposition, when Clinton insiders were pressed about the campaign's role in spreading the collusion narrative, Elias was present. Every time a witness was asked the critical questions—who ordered the dossier, who approved its dissemination, what was said inside the campaign's war room—Elias cut in, cloaking the answers under the impenetrable shield of privilege. He wasn't just a lawyer protecting a client; he was the firewall protecting an entire criminal enterprise.

What makes Elias so dangerous—and so central—is that he knows everything. He knows who inside the Clinton campaign greenlit the plan. He knows how the lies were laundered into the FBI and intelligence community. He knows how the media was spoon-fed its narratives, and how congressional allies like Adam Schiff were armed with talking points. He was present for it all. Pull that single thread—Marc Elias—and the entire hoax unravels.

And yet, like the rest of the architects, Elias has walked away untouched. The Administrative Mafia protects its fixers. He has gone on to wield even greater influence in Democratic politics, founding organizations, managing election-law battles, and continuing to shape the battlefield for his party. If Obama was the head of the snake, Elias was its spine. After Obama himself, Elias was the most significant figure in the Trump–Russia saga—the keystone who gave the hoax life, and the one man who still holds all its secrets.

This impunity is the scandal's final insult. It confirms what millions of Americans already suspect: that there is one standard of justice for the ruling class and another for everyone else. The Trump–Russia hoax was not just an assault on one man or one campaign—it was an attack on the very foundation of self-government. And the refusal to punish those responsible ensures the precedent remains alive, waiting to be used again. And it has been used against ordinary Americans.

Under the Biden Administration, the FBI targeted parents who dared to speak out at school board meetings as potential domestic threats, while weaponized investigations and selective prosecutions have multiplied across the political landscape. Pro-life activists have had their homes raided at gunpoint for minor protest-related charges. Catholic congregations have been monitored under the guise of investigating "extremism." January 6 defendants—many charged with nothing more than trespassing—have been treated as if they were enemy combatants. Even Trump's own lawyers, like Christina Bobb, have been dragged into criminal investigations simply for providing him legal counsel, a move that shatters the core principle of attorney–client privilege.

At the same time, political allies of the regime skate free from scrutiny. The pattern is unmistakable: the machinery of justice is no longer blind, but trained on those who challenge the ruling class, whether they are a president, a protester, or a parent. The 2016 Trump–Russia collusion hoax became a tyrannical template that paved the way for even greater abuses.

Having faced no consequences for weaponizing the FBI, DOJ, and intelligence community against a presidential candidate, the ruling elite have only grown more emboldened. Each abuse that went unpunished became a green light for the next. The lesson they drew from 2016 was not restraint, but opportunity. If they could attempt a coup through leaks and lies once, they could do it against anyone who dared to challenge their grip on power.

The intelligence community's meddling did not end with 2016. In the heat of the 2020 election, as the *New York Post* broke the story of Hunter Biden's abandoned laptop—a trove of emails, business records, and personal messages implicating the Biden family in questionable foreign dealings—the ruling elite moved swiftly to discredit it. Within days, fifty-one former intelligence officials signed a letter declaring that the laptop bore "all the classic earmarks of Russian disinformation." They knew it wasn't true. The letter's sole purpose was to give Joe Biden and his media allies a ready-made talking point to dismiss the scandal as another Russia plot. And it worked. The press and Big Tech censored the story, Biden invoked the letter to dodge questions during the debate, and millions of voters were left in the dark. On the heels of staging a failed coup against Trump in 2016, the ruling elite flipped the script in 2020, accusing Trump of the very crime they themselves had committed: undermining democracy.

In 2020, the United States broke with centuries of electoral tradition by rushing into unprecedented changes under the banner of COVID. Universal mail-in ballots were rolled out on a scale never before attempted in American history. Rules were rewritten at the last minute, deadlines stretched, signature verification loosened, and ballot-harvesting normalized. Every serious democracy in the world acknowledges that mass mail-in voting is uniquely vulnerable to fraud and abuse, which is why many nations ban it entirely or restrict it to narrow circumstances like overseas citizens or military personnel. Yet in 2020, America embraced it wholesale, opening the floodgates for chaos.

The result was predictable: millions of ballots floating outside the chain of custody, ballot drop boxes stuffed without meaningful oversight, and election procedures rewritten by courts and governors rather than legislatures. When Donald Trump questioned the legitimacy of an election carried out under these extraordinary conditions, the same ruling elite who had staged the Russia hoax in 2016 accused him of being anti-democracy.

As the 2024 election came into view, the ruling elite laid the groundwork to strip Donald Trump of his political life entirely, targeting him with criminal charges, raiding his Mar-a-Lago home, and unleashing grand juries over bogus crimes. In New York, Alvin Bragg indicted him on a laughable "hush money" bookkeeping case that would barely qualify as a misdemeanor if anyone else had done it. In Washington, Jack Smith brought charges over classified documents—despite presidents from Clinton to Biden hoarding government records without consequence—and then doubled down with another indictment accusing Trump of "conspiring to overturn the 2020 election," a political narrative dressed up as a crime. In Georgia, Fani Willis piled on with a sweeping Racketeer Influenced and Corrupt Organizations Act case that treated political speech and legal advice as criminal acts. Layered on top of this were endless civil suits, from Letitia James's crusade to dismantle his business empire to E. Jean Carroll's farcical defamation claims. It wasn't just about prosecution; it was about shutting down his candidacy, bankrupting his family, and silencing his movement. Yet even under the weight of these unprecedented legal assaults, public support for Trump remained remarkably resilient. To millions of voters, the raids and indictments weren't evidence of justice but proof of political warfare—confirmation that the same machinery that orchestrated 2016's Russia hoax was now fully weaponized to erase not just a man, but a movement.

President Trump survived it all—smear campaigns, hoaxes, prosecutions, raids, and even an attempt on his life. On July 13, 2024, at a rally in Butler, Pennsylvania, a gunman opened fire from a rooftop with an AR-15–style rifle. A bullet tore across Trump's right ear, killing a supporter and wounding others before the shooter was taken down by the Secret Service.

Just two months later, on September 15, another would-be assassin was discovered lying in wait at Trump's West Palm Beach club connected to Mar-a-Lago, armed with a rifle. Hidden among the brush, he was forced to flee when Secret Service agents opened fire. Twice in a single campaign season, the life of a former president—and leading candidate—was nearly taken.

These were not isolated events; they were the culmination of years of relentless attempts to destroy him. From the Russia hoax in 2016, to the impeachments, to the Mar-a-Lago raid, to criminal indictments designed to keep him off the ballot, every weapon of politics and lawfare had already been wielded. And when those failed, the attacks turned literal. Yet Trump endured. Bloodied but unbowed, he walked off the rally stage in Butler, Pennsylvania with his fist raised, defiant—a symbol to millions of Americans that their voice, and their vote, could not be silenced.

President Trump's miraculous victory—a testament to the greatness of America and to our distinct American spirit that refuses to yield—did not vanquish the enemy. The same forces that tried to frame, entrap, and destroy him remain entrenched in the halls of power, waiting for their next chance. His victory proved that the American people could still rise up against overwhelming odds—but it also revealed just how determined the ruling elite were to cling to power, no matter the cost to the republic.

As the Trump administration strives to restore the republic by finally bringing accountability to those in government who committed such egregious crimes against the country, those very criminals are working overtime to gaslight the public. They call investigations into their own misconduct "political retribution." They brand efforts to prosecute their abuses as "attacks on democracy." In truth, it is the ultimate inversion. The same officials who weaponized the state against a president and the American people now pretend they are the victims of persecution. Their strategy is as cynical as it is transparent—to delegitimize justice itself to escape it. Yet the more they scream, the more obvious it becomes that accountability is finally at their doorstep.

The Trump–Russia hoax was not an isolated scandal; it was the culmination of a long pattern that began years earlier. In Benghazi, the Obama administration and Hillary Clinton learned that they could lie to the American people, cover up their failures, and face no real consequences. The false narrative of a "video protest" was the trial run, a test to see if the ruling elite could rewrite reality itself. When they succeeded, they grew bolder. By 2016, the same cast of characters and their allies escalated to an even greater deception: the Russia collusion hoax, a coup in all but name, designed to destroy a political opponent and nullify the will of the voters.

From Benghazi to Crossfire Hurricane, the pattern is unmistakable. Each abuse built upon the last, each lie emboldened the next, until the peaceful transfer of power—the very cornerstone of the republic—was broken. And yet, America endured. Against dossiers, doctored evidence, weaponized investigations, impeachments, raids, and even assassination attempts, Donald Trump survived. More importantly, the people's voice survived. The defiance of Americans who refused to yield proved that the spirit of 1776 is not dead.

But the lesson of this long train of abuses is also clear: Unless those responsible are finally held to account, the cycle will continue. Benghazi was the beginning, the Russia hoax the escalation, and 2020 the proof that the ruling class will stop at nothing to preserve its power. The choice now belongs to the American people: to accept a government of lies, or to restore the republic their forefathers pledged their lives, fortunes, and sacred honor to defend.

It is time those in government fear the citizens, not the other way around. For only when power once again trembles before the people will the republic be restored, and only then will liberty endure.

ENDNOTES

1. Obama, Barack. "Coming Together to Remember September 11th." Weekly Address, The White House, 8 Sept. 2012, obamawhitehouse. archives.gov/the-press-office/2012/09/08/weekly-address-coming-together-remember-september-11th.

2. Ibid.

3. "U.S. Dog Bite Fatalities: Breeds of Dogs Involved, Age Groups and Other Factors Over a 13-Year Period (2005 to 2017)." DogsBite.org, May 2018, www.dogsbite.org/dog-bite-statistics-multi-year-fatality-report-2005-2017.php.

4. Obama, Barack. "Remarks by the President at National Prayer Breakfast." The White House, 5 Feb. 2015, obamawhitehouse.archives. gov/the-press-office/2015/02/05/remarks-president-national-prayer-breakfast.

5. Obama, Barack. "Remarks by the President at Islamic Society of Baltimore." The White House, 3 Feb. 2016, obamawhitehouse.archives. gov/the-press-office/2016/02/03/remarks-president-islamic-society-baltimore.

6. Ibid.

7. "Police Shootings Database: 10,429 People Have Been Shot and Killed by Police from 2015 to 2024." *The Washington Post*, www. washingtonpost.com/graphics/investigations/police-shootings-database/.

8. Tennessee General Assembly. *Senate Resolution No. 16.* 109th Gen. Assemb., 2016, publications.tnsosfiles.com/acts/109/resolutions/sr0016.pdf

9. Obama, Barack. Remarks by the President at the Closing of the Tribal Nations Conference. The White House, Office of the Press Secretary, 3 Nov. 2015, obamawhitehouse.archives.gov/the-press-office/ remarks-president-closing-tribal-nations-conference

10 Obama, Barack. Weekly Address: Tragedy at Fort Hood. The White House, 8 Nov. 2009, obamawhitehouse.archives.gov/photos-and-video/video/weekly-address-tragedy-fort-hood#transcript

11 Johnston, David, and Scott Shane. "U.S. Knew of Suspect's Tie to Radical Cleric." *The New York Times*, 10 Nov. 2009, www.nytimes.com/2009/11/10/us/10inquire.html.

12 Shane, Scott, comp. "The Anwar al-Awlaki File, Explained." National Security Archive, 14 Feb. 2025, nsarchive.gwu.edu/briefing-book/2025-02-14/anwar-al-awlaki-file-explained.

13 Webster Commission. "Final Report of the William H. Webster Commission on the FBI, Counterterrorism Intelligence, and the Events at Fort Hood, Texas, November 5, 2009." CNN via i2.cdn.turner.com (archived), 19 July 2012, web.archive.org/web/20140228200011/https://i2.cdn.turner.com/cnn/2012/images/07/19/william.webster.pdf.

14 Ibid.

15 "Connections Between Radical Cleric and Hasan Closely Examined." PBS NewsHour, 10 Nov. 2009, www.pbs.org/newshour/show/connections-between-radical-cleric-hasan-closely-examined.

16 Shane, Scott, and James Dao. "Investigators Study Tangle of Clues on Fort Hood Suspect." *The New York Times*, 14 Nov. 2009, www.nytimes.com/2009/11/15/us/15hasan.html.

17 Obama, Barack. "Weekly Address: President Obama Calls for Comprehensive Review of Events Leading to Tragedy at Fort Hood." The White House, 7 Nov. 2009, obamawhitehouse.archives.gov/the-press-office/weekly-address-president-obama-calls-comprehensive-review-events-leading-tragedy-fo.

18 Ibid.

19 "Protecting the Force: Lessons from Fort Hood." Report of the Department of Defense Independent Review, Jan. 2010, sgp.fas.org/eprint/fthood.pdf.

20 "Protecting the Force: Lessons from Fort Hood—DoD Report." Investigative Project on Terrorism, www.investigativeproject.org/case_docs/us-v-hasan-fort-hood-attack/1363/protecting-the-force-lessons-from-fort-hood-dod-report.pdf.

21 "Director Asks Judge Webster to Conduct Independent Review." FBI, archives.fbi.gov/archives/news/pressrel/press-releases/director-asks-judge-webster-to-conduct-independent-review.

22 Barnes, Steve, and James Dao. "Soldier Is Killed in Attack Outside Recruiting Station." *The New York Times*, 1 June 2009, www.nytimes.com/2009/06/02/us/02recruit.html.

23 Martinez, Edecio. "Suspect Says American Soldier's Murder Was
    Justified." CBS News, 10 June 2009, www.cbsnews.com/news/suspect-
    says-american-soldiers-murder-was-justified/.

24 National Threat Assessment Center. "Investigating Ideologically Inspired
    Violent Extremists: Local Partners Are an Asset—A Case Study on
    Abdulhakim Mujahid Muhammad." US Secret Service, Dec. 2015.

25 "Obama: 'Deeply Saddened' by Arkansas Shooting." CNN, 4 June 2009,
    www.cnn.com/2009/CRIME/06/04/obama.arkansas.shooting/.

26 Serrano, Richard A. "Federal Government Isn't Touching Arkansas
    Terrorism Case." *Los Angeles Times*, 11 July 2011, law.uark.edu/
    documents/gallini/gallini-7-11-11_--little_rock_shooting_-_los_angeles_
    times.pdf.

27 "Attorney General Lynch Statement Following the Federal Grand Jury
    Indictment Against Dylann Storm Roof." US Department of Justice, 22
    July 2015, www.justice.gov/archives/opa/pr/attorney-general-lynch-
    statement-following-federal-grand-jury-indictment-against-dylann-
    storm.

28 Office of the Secretary. "Remarks on Benghazi Attack." US Department
    of State, 14 Sept. 2012, 2009–2017.state.gov/secretary/20092013clinton/
    rm/2012/09/197654.htm.

29 Lister, Tim. "Diplomatic Cables Show Anxiety about Benghazi Violence,
    Protection Level." CNN, 19 Oct. 2012, www.cnn.com/2012/10/19/
    world/africa/benghazi-documents.

30 Lieberman, J. I. "A Special Report on the Terrorist Attack at Benghazi."
    United States Senate, Committee on Homeland Security and
    Governmental Affairs, 2012, irp.fas.org/congress/2012_rpt/benghazi.pdf

31 Sundby, Alex. "Ambassador Warned Libya Was 'Volatile and Violent'."
    CBS News, 19 Oct. 2012, www.cbsnews.com/news/ambassador-warned-
    libya-was-volatile-and-violent/?utm_source=chatgpt.com.

32 Herridge, Catherine. "Exclusive: Cable Warning of Benghazi Consulate
    Vulnerability Would Have Gone to White House, Officials Say." Fox
    News, 5 Nov. 2012, www.foxnews.com/politics/exclusive-cable-warning-
    of-benghazi-consulate-vulnerability-would-have-gone-to-white-house-
    officials-say.

33 McGreal, Chris. "Benghazi Attack Testimony Claims State Department
    Ignored Warnings." *The Guardian*, 10 Oct. 2012, www.theguardian.
    com/world/2012/oct/10/benghazi-attack-testimony-state-department.

34 United States, House Permanent Select Committee on Intelligence.
    "HPSCI January 2014 Update on Benghazi." Jan. 2014, intelligence.

house.gov/sites/intelligence.house.gov/files/documents/
hpscibenghaziupdatejan2014.pdf.

35 Al Shalchi, Hadeel. "In Libya, Deadly Fury Took U.S. Envoys by Surprise." *Reuters*, 13 Sept. 2012, www.reuters.com/article/world/us/in-libya-deadly-fury-took-us-envoys-by-surprise-idUSBRE88C02Q.

36 Schmitt, Eric. "C.I.A. Said to Aid in Steering Arms to Syrian Rebels." *The New York Times*, 21 June 2012, www.nytimes.com/2012/06/21/world/middleeast/cia-said-to-aid-in-steering-arms-to-syrian-rebels.html.

37 Browne, Pamela. "Was Syrian Weapons Shipment Factor in Ambassador's Benghazi Visit?" Fox News, 25 Oct. 2012, www.foxnews.com/politics/was-syrian-weapons-shipment-factor-in-ambassadors-benghazi-visit.

38 Frenkel, Sheera. "Syrian Rebels Squabble over Weapons as Biggest Shipload Arrives from Libya." *The Times* (London), 14 Sept. 2012, www.thetimes.com/travel/destinations/europe-travel/turkey/syrian-rebels-squabble-over-weapons-as-biggest-shipload-arrives-from-libya-pr2rmxkpg8d.

39 McElroy, Damien. "CIA 'Running Arms Smuggling Team in Benghazi When Consulate Was Attacked.'" *The Telegraph*, 1 Aug. 2013, https://www.telegraph.co.uk/news/worldnews/africaandindianocean/libya/10218288/CIA-running-arms-smuggling-team-in-Benghazi-when-consulate-was-attacked.html

40 "President Obama Official Schedule and Guidance, Sept. 11, 2012 – 9/11 Observance." *Chicago Sun-Times*, 19 Nov. 2013, chicago.suntimes.com/politics/2013/11/19/18547803/president-obama-official-schedule-and-guidance-sept-11-2012-9-11-observance.

41 Halper, Daniel. "Panetta: Obama Absent Night of Benghazi." *Washington Examiner*, 7 Feb. 2013, www.washingtonexaminer.com/policy/defense/1028256/panetta-obama-absent-night-of-benghazi.

42 Samuelsohn, Darren. "Obama Briefed Wed. of Ambassador's Death." *Politico*, 12 Sept. 2012, www.politico.com/blogs/politico44/2012/09/obama-briefed-wed-of-ambassadors-death-135279.

43 Bolton, John R. "Benghazi Bungle: Obama's Pass-the-Buck Presidency." AEI, 11 Feb. 2013, www.aei.org/articles/benghazi-bungle-obamas-pass-the-buck-presidency/.

44 Garamone, Jim. "President Obama Makes Case for U.S. Participation in Libya." Air Mobility Command, 29 Mar. 2011, www.amc.af.mil/News/Article-Display/Article/145823/president-obama-makes-case-for-us-participation-in-libya/.

45 "Pentagon Releases Official Timeline of Benghazi Attack." CNN, 9 Nov. 2012, www.cnn.com/2012/11/09/world/africa/libya-benghazi-timeline.

46 Hillary Clinton Email Archive. "Email from Hillary Clinton to 'Diane Reynolds,' 'I'm in my Office.'" Wikileaks, 11 Sept. 2012, wikileaks.org/clinton-emails/emailid/19611.

47 United States, Congress, House, "Select Committee on the Events Surrounding the 2012 Terrorist Attack in Benghazi. Final Report of the Select Committee on the Events Surrounding the 2012 Terrorist Attack in Benghazi." US Government Publishing Office, House Report No. 114–848, 114th Cong., 2d sess., 7 Dec. 2016, https://www.congress.gov/committee-report/114th-congress/house-report/848/1.

48 "Hillary Got Warning Benghazi Attack Was 'Premeditated Terrorism.'" *New York Post*, 21 May 2015, https://nypost.com/2015/05/21/hillary-got-warning-benghazi-attack-was-premeditated-terrorism/?utm_source=chatgpt.com.

49 Carroll, Rory. "Anti-Islamic Film Search Leads to Coptic Christian in California." *The Guardian*, 12 Sept. 2012, https://www.theguardian.com/world/2012/sep/13/anti-islamic-film-us-nakoula?utm_source=chatgpt.com.

50 Attkisson, Sharyl. "New Documents Reveal Events Leading Up to Benghazi Attack." *CBS News*, 1 Nov. 2012, https://www.cbsnews.com/news/new-documents-reveal-events-leading-up-to-benghazi-attack/.

51 Ibid.

52 Karl, Jonathan. "Exclusive: Benghazi Talking Points Underwent 12 Revisions, Scrubbed of Terror Reference." ABC News, 10 May 2013, https://abcnews.go.com/blogs/politics/2013/05/exclusive-benghazi-talking-points-underwent-12-revisions-scrubbed-of-terror-references.

53 Ibid.

54 "Media Observers on ABC's Jonathan Karl Benghazi Talking Points Story: 'Sloppy' and 'Inaccurate.'" Media Matters for America, 16 May 2013, https://www.mediamatters.org/abc/media-observers-abcs-jonathan-karl-benghazi-talking-points-story-sloppy-and-inaccurate.

55 Carney, Jay. "Press Briefing by Press Secretary Jay Carney, 05/14/2013." The White House, 14 May 2013, https://obamawhitehouse.archives.gov/the-press-office/2013/05/14/press-briefing-press-secretary-jay-carney-05142013.

56 Obama, Barack. "Remarks by the President on the Deaths of U.S. Embassy Staff in Libya." The White House, 12 Sept. 2012, https://obamawhitehouse.archives.gov/the-press-office/2012/09/12/remarks-president-deaths-us-embassy-staff-Libya.

57   Obama, Barack. "Address to the Nation by the President." The White House, 6 Dec. 2015, https://obamawhitehouse.archives.gov/the-press-office/2015/12/06/address-nation-president.

58   Associated Press. "Former Deputy CIA Director Defends Editing Benghazi Talking Points." *The Guardian*, 2 Apr. 2014, https://www.theguardian.com/world/2014/apr/02/cia-mike-morell-defends-benghazi-talking-points. Accessed 27 Sept. 2025.

59   House Committee on the Judiciary. "New Testimony Reveals Secretary Blinken and Biden Campaign Behind the Infamous Public Statement on the Hunter Biden Laptop." Press release, 20 Apr. 2023, https://judiciary.house.gov/media/press-releases/new-testimony-reveals-secretary-blinken-and-biden-campaign-behind-infamous.

60   Graham, Lindsey. "Statement By Graham, McCain and Ayotte On President Obama's Comments On Benghazi." Press release, 13 May 2013, https://www.lgraham.senate.gov/public/index.cfm/press-releases?ID=9F9FABF5-BA3D-1E27-99F5-8E226008F500.

61   United States, Congress, House, Select Committee on the Events Surrounding the 2012 Terrorist Attack in Benghazi. "Final Report of the Select Committee on the Events Surrounding the 2012 Terrorist Attack in Benghazi." US Government Publishing Office, House Report No. 114–848, 114th Cong., 2d sess., 7 Dec. 2016, https://www.congress.gov/114/crpt/hrpt848/CRPT-114hrpt848.pdf.

62   Gardner, Amy. "On Letterman, Obama Says Romney 'Writing Off' Much of Country." *The Washington Post,* 18 Sept. 2012, https://www.washingtonpost.com/politics/decision2012/on-letterman-obama-says-romney-writing-off-much-of-country/2012/09/18/645c8c04-01ba-11e2-b257-e1c2b3548a4a_story.html.

63   Memoli, Michael A. "Obama Responds to Romney Remarks in David Letterman Interview." *Los Angeles Times*, 18 Sept. 2012, https://www.latimes.com/entertainment/la-xpm-2012-sep-18-la-pn-obama-romney-david-letterman-20120918-story.html.

64   "President Addresses Controversial Romney Comments During Sit-Down With Letterman." CBS New York, 19 Sept. 2012, https://www.cbsnews.com/newyork/news/president-addresses-controversial-romney-comments-during-sit-down-with-letterman/.

65   Video: Obama's full interview on the 'Late Show with David Letterman.' *The Washington Post*, 18 Sept. 2012, https://www.washingtonpost.com/video/politics/decision2012/top-8-things-late-night-tv-has-taught-us-about-obama-and-the-first-lady/2012/09/18/90d1af64-01cc-11e2-b257-e1c2b3548a4a_video.html.

66 "President Obama's Interview on 'The Late Show with David Letterman'." *The Washington Post*, 19 Sept. 2012, https://www. washingtonpost.com/video/president-obamas-interview-on-the-late-show-with-david-letterman/2012/09/19/ef906ff8-0227-11e2-bbf0-e33b4ee2f0e8_video.html.

67 Farhi, Paul. "How Mother Jones Got the Romney '47-Percent' Story." *The Washington Post*, 18 Sept. 2012, https://www.washingtonpost.com/lifestyle/style/how-a-mother-jones-reporter-pursued-the-romney-47-percent-story/2012/09/18/c6dc17e8-01d1-11e2-b257-e1c2b3548a4a_story.html.

68 Obama, Barack. "Remarks by the President at Univision Town Hall with Jorge Ramos and Maria Elena Salinas." The White House, 20 Sept. 2012, https://obamawhitehouse.archives.gov/the-press-office/2012/09/20/remarks-president-univision-town-hall-jorge-ramos-and-maria-elena-salina.

69 "2012 Presidential Debate: Full Transcript (Oct. 16)." ABC News, 16 Oct.2012,https://abcnews.go.com/Politics/OTUS/2012-presidential-debate-full-transcript-oct-16/story?id=17493848.

70 Ibid.

71 Ibid.

72 "Moderator Crowley Says Romney 'Right in the Main' on Libya, Despite Debate Intervention." Fox News, 17 Oct. 2012, https://www.foxnews.com/politics/moderator-crowley-says-romney-right-in-the-main-on-libya-despite-debate-intervention.

73 Politico Staff. "Transcript: Third presidential debate." *Politico*, 22 Oct. 2012, https://www.politico.com/story/2012/10/third-debate-transcript-082712.

74 Lieberman, Joseph I. "Report on the Terrorist Attack at Benghazi." Congressional Record: Proceedings and Debates of the 112th Congress, vol. 158, no. 170 (Senate), 30 Dec. 2012, pp. S8530–S8541. GovInfo, https://www.govinfo.gov/content/pkg/CREC-2012-12-30/html/CREC-2012-12-30-pt1-PgS8530-5.htm.

75 Clinton, Hillary. "Remarks With Pakistani Foreign Minister Hina Rabbani Khar." US Department of State, 21 Sept. 2012, https://2009-2017.state.gov/secretary/20092013clinton/rm/2012/09/198060.htm.

76 Graham, Lindsey. "Statement By Graham, McCain and Ayotte On President Obama's Comments On Benghazi." Press release, 13 May 2013, https://www.lgraham.senate.gov/public/index.cfm/press-releases?ID=9F9FABF5-BA3D-1E27-99F5-8E226008F500.

77   Judicial Watch. "Judicial Watch Sues Obama State Department for Benghazi Attack Videos and Photographs." GlobeNewswire, 5 Mar. 2013, https://www.globenewswire.com/news-release/2013/03/05/1046855/0/en/Judicial-Watch-Sues-Obama-State-Department-for-Benghazi-Attack-Videos-and-Photographs.html.

78   Ibid.

79   Judicial Watch. "Ben Rhodes Benghazi Email." Judicial Watch, 17 Apr. 2014, https://www.judicialwatch.org/wp-content/uploads/2014/06/Rhodes-Email.pdf.

80   Schmidt, Michael S. "Hillary Clinton's Use of Private Email at State Dept. Raises Flags." *The New York Times*, 3 Mar. 2015, https://www.nytimes.com/2015/03/03/us/politics/hillary-clintons-use-of-private-email-at-state-department-raises-flags.html.

81   Gordon, Greg. "Hillary Clinton Got Nearly $1.6 Million from Big Banks in 2013." *The Miami Herald*, 6 Aug. 2015, www.miamiherald.com/news/nation-world/national/article29716723.html.

82   O'Harrow, Robert, Jr. "How Clinton's Email Scandal Took Root." *The Washington Post*, 27 Mar. 2016, www.washingtonpost.com/investigations/how-clintons-email-scandal-took-root/2016/03/27/ee301168-e162-11e5-846c-10191d1fc4ec_story.html.

83   United States, Department of Justice, Office of the Inspector General. A Review of Various Actions by the Federal Bureau of Investigation and the Department of Justice in Advance of the 2016 Election. June 14, 2018. PDF file, int.nyt.com/data/documenthelper/39-justice-department-report-fbi-clinton-comey/5e54a6bfd23e7b94fbad/optimized/full.pdf

84   Comey, James B. "Statement by FBI Director James B. Comey on the Investigation of Secretary Hillary Clinton's Use of a Personal E-Mail System." FBI, 5 July 2016, www.fbi.gov/news/press-releases/statement-by-fbi-director-james-b-comey-on-the-investigation-of-secretary-hillary-clinton2019s-use-of-a-personal-e-mail-system.

85   "A Timeline of Hillary Clinton's Email Saga." ABC News, 7 Nov. 2016, abcnews.go.com/Politics/timeline-hillary-clintons-email-saga/story?id=29442707.

86   Flores, Reena. "Obama Weighs in on Hillary Clinton's Private Emails." CBS News, 7 Mar. 2015, www.cbsnews.com/news/obama-weighs-in-hillary-clinton-private-emails/.

87   Wright, Andy. "What Does the Presidential Records Act Have to Say About Private Email Use?" *Just Security*, 9 Oct. 2017, https://www.justsecurity.org/45764/whadoes-presidential-records-act-private-email-use/

88 Presidential and Federal Records Act Amendments of 2014, Pub. L. 113–187, 128 Stat. 2009, 26 Nov. 2014.

89 Sullivan, Margaret. "Obama Promised Transparency. But His Administration Is One of the Most Secretive." *The Washington Post*, 24 May 2016, www.washingtonpost.com/lifestyle/style/obama-promised-transparency-but-his-administration-is-one-of-the-most-secretive/2016/05/24/5a46caba-21c1-11e6-9e7f-57890b612299_story.html.

90 National Archives. "Presidential Records Act (PRA) of 1978." National Archives and Records Administration, www.archives.gov/presidential-libraries/laws/1978-act.html.

91 Landler, Mark. "Lost in Translation: A U.S. Gift to Russia." *The New York Times*, 6 Mar. 2009, www.nytimes.com/2009/03/07/world/europe/07diplo.html.

92 Nelson, Louis. "Hillary Clinton, Russia, and Uranium: What You Need to Know." *Politico*, 14 Nov. 2017, www.politico.com/story/2017/11/14/hillary-clinton-uranium-one-deal-russia-explainer-244895.

93 Becker, Jo, and Mike McIntire. "Cash Flowed to Clinton Foundation as Russians Pressed for Control of Uranium Company." *The New York Times*, 23 Apr. 2015, www.nytimes.com/2015/04/24/us/cash-flowed-to-clinton-foundation-as-russians-pressed-for-control-of-uranium-company.html.

94 Solomon, John. "Uranium One Informant Makes Clinton Allegations in Testimony." *The Hill*, 17 Jan. 2018, thehill.com/homenews/administration/372861-uranium-one-informant-makes-clinton-allegations-in-testimony/

95 Baker, Peter, and Nicholas Kulish. "White House Scraps Bush Plan for Missile Defense in Europe." *The New York Times*, 17 Sept. 2009, www.nytimes.com/2009/09/18/world/europe/18shield.html. Accessed 28 Sept. 2025.

96 "State of the Union with Jake Tapper." Interview with Robby Mook. CNN Press Room, 24 July 2016, cnnpressroom.blogs.cnn.com/2016/07/24/mook-on-dnc-e-mail-leak-experts-are-now-saying-that-the-russians-are-releasing-these-e-mails-for-the-purpose-of-actually-helping-donald-trump.

97 Swaine, Jon. "Clinton on Email Controversy: 'Would Have Been Better' to Use Two Accounts." *The Guardian*, 10 Mar. 2015, www.theguardian.com/us-news/2015/mar/10/hillary-clinton-email-scandal-un-press-conference.

98 "Meet the Press—July 3, 2016." NBC News, nbcnews.com/meet-the-press/meet-press-july-3-2016-n603166.

99   Comey, James B. "Statement by FBI Director James B. Comey on the Investigation of Secretary Hillary Clinton's Use of a Personal E-Mail System." FBI, 5 July 2016, www.fbi.gov/news/press-releases/statement-by-fbi-director-james-b-comey-on-the-investigation-of-secretary-hillary-clinton2019s-use-of-a-personal-e-mail-system.

100 Henry, Shawn. "Testimony of Shawn Henry, President, CrowdStrike Services." House Permanent Select Committee on Intelligence, 5 Dec. 2017, intelligence.house.gov/uploadedfiles/shawn_henry_testimony_dec_5_2017.pdf.

101 "Julian Assange: 'Our Source Is Not the Russian Government.'" Fox News, 3 Jan. 2017, www.foxnews.com/transcript/julian-assange-our-source-is-not-the-russian-government. Accessed 28 Sept. 2025.

102 Mueller, Robert S., III. "Report on the Investigation into Russian Interference in the 2016 Presidential Election." Vol. I, US Department of Justice, 18 Apr. 2019, www.justice.gov/storage/report.pdf.

103 Davies, Nick, and David Leigh. "Afghanistan War Logs: Massive Leak of Secret Files Exposes Truth of Occupation." *The Guardian*, 25 July 2010, www.theguardian.com/world/2010/jul/25/afghanistan-war-logs-military-leaks.

104 Tran, Mark. "WikiLeaks to Publish More Hillary Clinton Emails—Julian Assange." *The Guardian*, 12 June 2016, www.theguardian.com/media/2016/jun/12/wikileaks-to-publish-more-hillary-clinton-emails-julian-assange.

105 Nakashima, Ellen. "Russian Government Hackers Penetrated DNC, Stole Opposition Research on Trump." *The Washington Post*, 14 June 2016, www.washingtonpost.com/world/national-security/russian-government-hackers-penetrated-dnc-stole-opposition-research-on-trump/2016/06/14/cf006cb4-316e-11e6-8ff7-7b6c1998b7a0_story.html.

106 Peterson, Andrea. "Wikileaks posts nearly 20,000 hacked DNC emails online." *The Washington Post*, 22 July 2016, www.washingtonpost.com/news/the-switch/wp/2016/07/22/wikileaks-posts-nearly-20000-hacked-dnc-emails-online/.

107 Fahrenthold, David A. "Trump Recorded Having Extremely Lewd Conversation About Women in 2005." *The Washington Post*, 7 Oct. 2016, www.washingtonpost.com/politics/trump-recorded-having-extremely-lewd-conversation-about-women-in-2005/2016/10/07/3b9ce776-8cb4-11e6-bf8a-3d26847eeed4_story.html.

108 Guthrie, Mareesa, and Susan Seager. "Why NBC Sat on the 'Access Hollywood' Trump Tape." *LAist*, 10 Oct. 2016, laist.com/shows/the-frame/why-nbc-sat-on-the-access-hollywood-trump-tape.

109 Helderman, Rosalind S., Tom Hamburger, Kevin Uhrmacher, and John Muyskens. "What We Know About the Steele Dossier's Origins." *The Washington Post*, 2018, www.washingtonpost.com/graphics/2018/politics/steele-timeline/#:~:text=Christopher%20Steele%20is%20a%20British,Donald%20Trump's%20ties%20to%20Russia.

110 Bensinger, Ken, Miriam Elder, and Mark Schoofs. "These Reports Allege Trump Has Deep Ties to Russia." *BuzzFeed News*, 10 Jan. 2017, www.buzzfeednews.com/article/kenbensinger/these-reports-allege-trump-has-deep-ties-to-russia.

111 Mosk, Matthew, Lucien Bruggeman, and Chris Donovan. "Behind the Dossier: How Christopher Steele Penned His Reports—and the Fallout from His Unmasking." ABC News, 15 Oct. 2021, abcnews.go.com/US/dossier-christopher-steele-penned-reports-fallout-unmasking/story?id=80536926.

112 "Declassified Durham Annex Released by Chairman Grassley." Grassley.senate.gov, www.grassley.senate.gov/imo/media/doc/declassified_durham_annex_released_by_chairman_grassley.pdf.

113 Ibid.

114 "The Clinton Foundation Meeting Timeline." *Just The News*, 2025, justthenews.com/sites/default/files/2025-08/Clinton%20Foundation%20Timeline.pdf.

115 Vogel, Kenneth P. "Clinton Campaign and DNC Helped Pay for Russia Dossier." *The New York Times*, 24 Oct. 2017, www.nytimes.com/2017/10/24/us/politics/clinton-dnc-russia-dossier.html.

116 Zapotosky, Matt. "Attorney General Meets with Former President Clinton amid Politically Charged Investigation into His Wife's Email." *The Washington Post*, 30 June 2016, www.washingtonpost.com/news/post-nation/wp/2016/06/29/attorney-general-meets-with-former-president-clinton-amid-politically-charged-investigation-into-his-wifes-email/.

117 Sign, Christopher. "US Attorney General Loretta Lynch, Bill Clinton Meet Privately in Phoenix before Benghazi Report." ABC15 Arizona, 29 June 2016, www.abc15.com/news/region-phoenix-metro/central-phoenix/us-attorney-general-loretta-lynch-bill-clinton-meet-privately-in-phoenix-before-benghazi-report.

118 Siddiqui, Sabrina, and Martin Pengelly. "Hillary Clinton Was 'Eager' for FBI Interview on Use of Private Email Server." *The Guardian*, 3 July

2016, www.theguardian.com/us-news/2016/jul/02/
hillary-clinton-interviewed-fbi-emails.

119 Comey, James B. "Statement by FBI Director James B. Comey on the
Investigation of Secretary Hillary Clinton's Use of a Personal E-Mail
System." FBI, 5 July 2016, www.fbi.gov/news/press-releases/
statement-by-fbi-director-james-b-comey-on-the-investigation-of-
secretary-hillary-clinton2019s-use-of-a-personal-e-mail-system.

120 Ibid.

121 Ibid.

122 Peterson, Andrea. "WikiLeaks Posts Nearly 20,000 Hacked DNC Emails
Online." *The Washington Post*, 22 July 2016, www.washingtonpost.com/
news/the-switch/wp/2016/07/22/wikileaks-posts-nearly-20000-hacked-
dnc-emails-online/.

123 Ratcliffe, John. "Letter to Sen. Lindsey Graham: Declassification of
Certain Intelligence Community Information Related to the FBI's
Crossfire Hurricane Investigation." 29 Sept. 2020, judiciary.senate.gov/
imo/media/doc/09-29-20_Letter%20to%20Sen.%20Graham_
Declassification%20of%20FBI%27s%20Crossfire%20Hurricane%20
Investigations_20-00912_U_SIGNED-FINAL.pdf.

124 United States Senate, Office of Senator Chuck Grassley. "Crossfire
Hurricane Timeline with Updates." 3 Dec. 2020, www.grassley.senate.
gov/imo/media/doc/CFH%20Timeline%20w%20Updates%20
20201203%20(FINAL).pdf.

125 Perez, Evan. "Sources: US Officials Warned DNC of Hack Months
before the Party Acted." CNN, 25 July 2016, www.cnn.com/2016/
07/25/politics/democratic-convention-dnc-emails-russia.

126 Sanger, David E., and Nicole Perlroth. "Russian Hackers Read Obama's
Unclassified Emails, Officials Say." *The New York Times*, 26 Apr. 2015,
www.nytimes.com/2015/04/26/us/russian-hackers-read-obamas-
unclassified-emails-officials-say.html.

127 Ibid.

128 Hosenball, Mark, and John Walcott. "Exclusive: Congressional Leaders
Were Briefed a Year Ago on Hacking of Democrats." *Reuters*, 12 Aug.
2016, www.reuters.com/article/world/exclusive-congressional-leaders-
were-briefed-a-year-ago-on-hacking-of-democrats-idUSKCN10N00C/.

129 Greenberg, Andy. "The FBI Botched Its DNC Hack Warning in
2016—but Says It Won't Next Time." *Wired*, 2 Sept. 2020, www.wired.
com/story/fbi-hacking-victim-notifications/.

130 Tamene, Yared Wolde Yohannes. "Testimony of Yared Tamene Wolde
Yohannes before the House Permanent Select Committee on

Intelligence." 30 Aug. 2017, intelligence.house.gov/uploadedfiles/
yared_tamene_wolde_yohannes_testimony_aug_30_2017.pdf.

131   Ibid.

132   Ibid.

133   "FBI Response to Committee Questions for the Record." United States
Senate, Select Committee on Intelligence, intelligence.senate.gov/
wp-content/uploads/2024/08/sites-default-files-documents-fbi-response-
to-committee-questions-for-the-record.pdf.

134   Tamene, Yared Wolde Yohannes. "Testimony of Yared Tamene Wolde
Yohannes before the House Permanent Select Committee on
Intelligence," 30 Aug. 2017, intelligence.house.gov/uploadedfiles/
yared_tamene_wolde_yohannes_testimony_aug_30_2017.pdf.

135   Ibid.

136   Ibid.

137   Ibid.

138   Ibid.

139   Ibid.

140   Ibid.

141   CrowdStrike Editorial Team. *CrowdStrike's Work with the Democratic
National Committee: Setting the Record Straight.* CrowdStrike, 4 June
2020, https://www.crowdstrike.com/en-us/blog/bears-midst-intrusion-
democratic-national-committee/

142   Sanger, David E., and Nick Corasaniti. "D.N.C. Says Russian Hackers
Penetrated Its Files, Including Dossier on Donald Trump." *The New York
Times*, 14 June 2016, www.nytimes.com/2016/06/15/us/politics/
russian-hackers-dnc-trump.html.

143   Ibid.

144   Strauss, Daniel. "Russian Government Hackers Broke into DNC Servers,
Stole Trump Oppo." *Politico*, 14 June 2016, www.politico.com/
story/2016/06/russian-government-hackers-broke-into-dnc-servers-
stole-trump-oppo-224315.

145   "Democrat hack: Who is Guccifer 2.0?" BBC News, 28 July 2016, www.
bbc.com/news/technology-36913000.

146   "'Lone Hacker' Claims Responsibility for Cyber Attack on Democrats."
Reuters, 16 June 2016, www.reuters.com/article/world/lone-hacker-claims-
responsibility-for-cyber-attack-on-democrats-idUSKCN0Z209W/.

147   Collinson, Stephen. "Hillary Clinton Clinches Democratic Presidential
Nomination." CNN, 6 June 2016, www.cnn.com/2016/06/06/politics/
hillary-clinton-nomination-2016.

148 "Update on Sony Investigation." FBI, 19 Dec. 2014, www.fbi.gov/news/press-releases/update-on-sony-investigation.

149 Naval Criminal Investigative Service. "Joint Investigation Leads to Indictments of Chinese Nationals for Computer Hacking Campaign." NCIS News, 5 Mar. 2025, www.ncis.navy.mil/Media/News/Article/4108434/joint-investigation-leads-to-indictments-of-chinese-nationals-for-computer-hack/.

150 "Chinese Hackers Charged in Equifax Breach." FBI, 10 Feb. 2020, www.fbi.gov/news/stories/chinese-hackers-charged-in-equifax-breach-021020.

151 *Chinese Military Hackers Charged in Equifax Breach.* FBI, 10 Feb. 2020, https://www.fbi.gov/news/stories/chinese-hackers-charged-in-equifax-breach-021020

152 Hosenball, Mark, and John Walcott. "Exclusive: Congressional Leaders Were Briefed a Year Ago on Hacking of Democrats." *Reuters*, 12 Aug. 2016, www.reuters.com/article/world/exclusive-congressional-leaders-were-briefed-a-year-ago-on-hacking-of-democrats-idUSKCN10N00C/.

153 United States Senate, Chuck Grassley, Chairman. "Declassified Durham Annex Released by Chairman Grassley." Senate Judiciary Committee, 2025, www.grassley.senate.gov/imo/media/doc/declassified_durham_annex_released_by_chairman_grassley.pdf.

154 Ibid.

155 Ibid.

156 Frizell, Sam, and Zeke J. Miller. "Exclusive: Conservative Group Calls for Federal Inquiry Into Hillary Clinton Son-in-Law Request." *Time Magazine*, 13 Dec. 2015, time.com/4147115/hillary-clinton-emails-marc-mezvinsky/.

157 United States Senate, Chuck Grassley, Chairman. "Declassified Durham Annex Released by Chairman Grassley." Senate Judiciary Committee, 2025, www.grassley.senate.gov/imo/media/doc/declassified_durham_annex_released_by_chairman_grassley.pdf.

158 Ibid.

159 Ibid.

160 United States, Department of Justice. "Report on Matters Related to Intelligence Activities and Investigations Arising Out of the 2016 Presidential Campaigns (Durham Report)." 12 May 2023, www.justice.gov/storage/durhamreport.pdf.

161 Singman, Brooke. "DNI Declassifies Brennan Notes, CIA Memo on Hillary Clinton 'Stirring Up' Scandal Between Trump, Russia." Fox News, 6 Oct. 2020, www.foxnews.com/politics/dni-brennan-notes-cia-memo-clinton.

162 "The Clinton Foundation Meeting Timeline." *Just the News*, Oct. 17, 2017, justthenews.com/sites/default/files/2025-08/Clinton%20 Foundation%20Timeline.pdf.

163 United States Senate, Chuck Grassley, Chairman. "Declassified Durham Annex Released by Chairman Grassley." Senate Judiciary Committee, 2025, www.grassley.senate.gov/imo/media/doc/declassified_durham_ annex_released_by_chairman_grassley.pdf.

164 Ibid.

165 NPR Staff. "READ: IG Report From Justice Department on the Russia Investigation." NPR, 9 Dec. 2019, www.npr.org/2019/12/09/ 785213175/read-doj-inspector-generals-report-on-the-russia-investigation.

166 Thompson, Alex. "Durham Report Takeaways." *Politico*, 15 May 2023, www.politico.com/news/2023/05/15/durham-report-takeaways-00097060.

167 United States, Department of Justice, Office of Inspector General. "Review of Four FISA Applications and Other Aspects of the FBI's Crossfire Hurricane Investigation." Dec. 2019, www.justice.gov/ storage/120919-examination.pdf.

168 Cohen, Zachary, Devan Cole, Tierney Sneed, Evan Perez, Hannah Rabinowitz, Jeremy Herb, and Marshall Cohen. "Special Counsel John Durham Concludes FBI Never Should Have Launched Full Trump-Russia Probe." CNN, 15 May 2023, edition.cnn.com/2023/05/15/ politics/john-durham-report-fbi-trump-released.

169 Demirjian, Karoun, and Devlin Barrett. "How a Dubious Russian Document Influenced the FBI's Handling of the Clinton Probe." *The Washington Post*, 24 May 2017, www.washingtonpost.com/world/ national-security/how-a-dubious-russian-document-influenced-the-fbis-handling-of-the-clinton-probe/2017/05/24/f375c07c-3a95-11e7-9e48-c4f199710b69_story.html.

170 United States Senate, Chuck Grassley, Chairman. "Declassified Durham Annex Released by Chairman Grassley." Senate Judiciary Committee, 2025, www.grassley.senate.gov/imo/media/doc/declassified_durham_ annex_released_by_chairman_grassley.pdf.

171 Ibid.

172 United States Senate, Senate Judiciary Committee. "Interview of Glenn Simpson (Redacted Transcript)." 22 Aug. 2017, www.judiciary.senate. gov/imo/media/doc/Simpson%20Transcript_redacted.pdf.

173 Entous, Adam, Devlin Barrett, and Rosalind S. Helderman. "Clinton Campaign, DNC Paid for Research That Led to Russia Dossier." *The*

Washington Post, 24 Oct. 2017, www.washingtonpost.com/world/
national-security/clinton-campaign-dnc-paid-for-research-that-led-to-
russia-dossier/2017/10/24/226fabf0-b8e4-11e7-a908-a3470754bbb9_
story.html.

174 United States Senate, Chuck Grassley, Chairman. "Declassified Durham
Annex Released by Chairman Grassley." Senate Judiciary Committee,
2025, www.grassley.senate.gov/imo/media/doc/declassified_durham_
annex_released_by_chairman_grassley.pdf.

175 Ibid.

176 Ibid.

177 Beckwith, Ryan Teague. "Read the Transcript of James Comey's
Testimony." *TIME*, 8 June 2017, https://time.com/4810345/james-
comey-testimony-real-time-transcript/

178 Ibid.

179 Ibid.

180 Ibid.

181 Ibid.

182 Ibid.

183 Ibid.

184 Ibid.

185 Ibid.

186 United States Department of Justice, Office of the Inspector General.
Review of Four FISA Applications and Other Aspects of the FBI's
Crossfire Hurricane Investigation. Dec. 2019, www.justice.gov/
storage/120919-examination.pdf.

187 LaFraniere, Sharon, Mark Mazzetti, and Matt Apuzzo. "How the Russia
Investigation Began: A Campaign Aide, Drinks and Talk of Political
Dirt." *The New York Times*, 30 Dec. 2017, www.nytimes.com/
2017/12/30/us/politics/how-fbi-russia-investigation-began-george-
papadopoulos.html.

188 Harding, Luke, Stephanie Kirchgaessner, and Shaun Walker. "George
Papadopoulos: Trump Adviser and the Lies About Russia." *The
Guardian*, 30 Oct. 2017, www.theguardian.com/us-news/2017/oct/30/
george-papadopoulos-donald-trump-russia-charge-putin.

189 McCarthy, Andrew C. "FBI Used False Premise to Open Trump-Russia
Investigation." *National Review*, 6 May 2019, www.nationalreview.
com/2019/05/fbi-trump-russia-investigation-george-papadopoulos/.

190 Ibid.

191 Ibid.

192 Greene, Andrew. "US Spy Boss James Robert Clapper Jr Makes Secretive Visit to Australia." ABC News, 16 Mar. 2016, www.abc.net.au/news/2016-03-16/us-spy-boss-makes-secretive-visit-to-australia/7251590.

193 Bradner, Eric. "Clinton's Campaign Manager: Russia Helping Trump." CNN, 24 July 2016, www.cnn.com/2016/07/24/politics/robby-mook-russia-dnc-emails-trump.

194 Helderman, Rosalind S., Tom Hamburger, Kevin Uhrmacher, and John Muyskens. "Timeline: How the Steele Dossier Was Compiled." *The Washington Post*, 6 Feb. 2018, www.washingtonpost.com/graphics/2018/politics/steele-timeline/.

195 United States, Department of Justice, Special Counsel's Office. "Report on the Investigation into Russian Interference in the 2016 Presidential Election." Vol. II, redacted version released 18 Apr. 2019, www.justsecurity.org/wp-content/uploads/2019/04/Muelller-Report-Redacted-Vol-II-Released-04.18.2019-Word-Searchable.-Reduced-Size.pdf.

196 "Trump Associate Denies Being 'Middle Man' to Russia." ABC News, 5 Dec. 2016, abcnews.go.com/Politics/trump-associate-denies-middle-man-russia/story?id=45206444.

197 United States, Department of Justice, Special Counsel's Office. "Report on the Investigation into Russian Interference in the 2016 Presidential Election." Vol. I, 18 Apr. 2019, www.justice.gov/storage/report.pdf.

198 Savage, Charlie. "Justice Dept. Says Facts Did Not Justify Continued Wiretap of Trump Aide." *The New York Times*, 23 Jan. 2020, www.nytimes.com/2020/01/23/us/politics/carter-page-fbi-surveillance.html.

199 Grassley, Chuck. "On the Inspector General Report on Russia Investigation and FISA." US Senate, Grassley News Releases, 10 Dec. 2019, www.grassley.senate.gov/news/news-releases/inspector-general-report-russia-investigation-and-fisa.

200 United States Senate Committee on the Judiciary. "Newly Declassified FBI Document Proves Fusion GPS Contractor Nellie Ohr Lied to Congress about Contributions to Crossfire Hurricane." US Senate, Judiciary Committee, 28 May 2025, www.judiciary.senate.gov/press/rep/releases/newly-declassified-fbi-document-proves-fusion-gps-contractor-nellie-ohr-lied-to-congress-about-contributions-to-crossfire-hurricane.

201 Christenson, Josh. "Nellie Ohr, Justice Department Official's Wife, Perjured Herself with 'Demonstrably False' Trump-Russia Testimony: Bombshell FBI Records." *New York Post*, 28 May 2025, nypost.com/2025/05/28/us-news/nellie-ohr-perjured-herself-in-trump-russia-probe-testimony-bombshell-fbi-records-show/

202 Rosiak, Luke. "EXCLUSIVE: DOJ Official Bruce Ohr Hid Wife's Fusion GPS Payments From Ethics Officials." *The Daily Caller*, 14 Feb. 2018, dailycaller.com/2018/02/14/exclusive-doj-official-bruce-ohr-hid-wifes-fusion-gps-payments-from-ethics-officials/.

203 Savage, Charlie, Adam Goldman, and Jonah M. Kessel. "Analyst Who Reported the Infamous Trump Tape Rumor Wants to Clear His Name." *The New York Times*, 21 Oct. 2020, www.nytimes.com/2020/10/21/us/politics/igor-danchenko-steele-dossier.html.

204 Dukakis, Ali. "'Steele Dossier 'Collector' Found Not Guilty on All Counts." ABC News, 18 Oct. 2022, abcnews.go.com/US/jury-begins-deliberations-case-steele-dossier-collector/story?id=91642931.

205 Weingarten, Ben. "FBI Paid for Russian Disinformation While Punishing Patriots." *Newsweek*, 22 Aug. 2022, www.newsweek.com/fbi-paid-russian-disinformation-while-punishing-patriot-opinion-1745574.

206 Chamberlain, Samuel, and Victor Nava. "Steele Dossier Source Igor Danchenko Acquitted of Lying to FBI." *New York Post*, 18 Oct. 2022, nypost.com/2022/10/18/steele-dossier-source-igor-danchenko-acquitted-of-lying-to-fbi/.

207 Isikoff, Michael. "U.S. Intel Officials Probe Ties Between Trump Adviser and Kremlin." Yahoo News, 23 Sept. 2016, www.yahoo.com/news/u-s-intel-officials-probe-ties-between-trump-advisor-and-kremlin-175046002.html.

208 *Minority Views on the Russia Investigation: Materials Relating to the June 9, 2016 Trump Tower Meeting*. U.S. House Committee on the Judiciary, 11 Dec. 2019, docs.house.gov/meetings/JU/JU00/20191211/110331/HMKP-116-JU00-20191211-SD052.pdf

209 Grand Jury Indicts D.C. Attorney with Making False Statements to the FBI in 2016 Regarding Alleged Communications Between Trump Organization and Russian Bank. U.S. Department of Justice, Special Counsel John Durham, 16 Sept. 2021, justice.gov/archives/sco/pr/grand-jury-indicts-dc-attorney-making-false-statements-fbi-2016-regarding-alleged

210 New Evidence Uncovers Obama-Directed Creation of False Intelligence Report Used to Launch Years-long Coup to Undermine President Trump and the American People. Office of the Director of National Intelligence, Press Release No. 18-25, 23 July 2025, dni.gov/index.php/newsroom/press-releases/press-releases-2025/4090-pr-18-25.

211 Office of the Director of National Intelligence. *Declassified Report: Manufactured Russia Hoax*. Office of the Director of National

Intelligence, July 2025, www.dni.gov/files/ODNI/documents/DIG/
DIG-Declassified-HPSCI-Report-Manufactured-Russia-Hoax-July2025.
pdf

212 *Tradecraft Review: 2016 ICA on Election Interference. Central Intelligence
Agency*, 25 June 2025, cia.gov/static/Tradecraft-Review-2016-ICA-on-
Election-Interference-062625.pdf.

213 ibid

214 United States. Congress. House. Committee on the Judiciary. *Oversight
of the Department of Justice*. 115th Cong., 2nd sess., 2018, govinfo.gov,
www.govinfo.gov/content/pkg/CHRG-115hhrg32476/html/CHRG-
115hhrg32476.htm

215 Associated Press. *"Read the Transcripts of Michael Flynn's Calls with
Russian Diplomat." PBS NewsHour*, 29 May 2020, https://www.pbs.org/
newshour/politics/read-the-transcripts-of-michael-flynns-calls-with-
russian-diplomat

216 *Michael Flynn's lawyers seize on note showing how FBI official approached
key interview.* **CNN**, 29 Apr. 2020, https://www.cnn.com/2020/04/29/
politics/flynn-note-fbi-interview/index.html. Accessed 15 Dec. 2025

217 Herb, Jeremy, Laura Jarrett, Manu Raju, Marshall Cohen, and David
Shortell. *"James Comey Defends FBI's Interview of Michael Flynn,
Transcript Shows."* **CNN**, 18 Dec. 2018, https://www.cnn.
com/2018/12/18/politics/james-comey-congress-interview/index.html

218 Northam, Jackie. *"Obama Expels 35 Diplomats, Imposes Retaliatory
Sanctions Against Russia for Hacking."* **NPR**, 29 Dec. 2016, https://www.
npr.org/2016/12/29/507436692/obama-expels-35-diplomats-
imposes-retaliatory-sanctions-against-russia-for-hacki

219 Foran, Clare. *"FBI Agent Peter Strzok Explains Why He Sent Anti-Trump
Text."* **CNN**, 12 July 2018, https://www.cnn.com/2018/07/12/politics/
strzok-testimony-text-message/index.html

220 Nava, Victor. *"Feds Investigating Sen. Adam Schiff for Alleged Mortgage
Fraud After DOJ Criminal Referral: Report." New York Post*, 5 Aug. 2025,
https://nypost.com/2025/08/05/us-news/sen-adam-schiff-under-
federal-criminal-investigation-for-alleged-mortgage-fraud-violations/

221 Rubin, Olivia, and Aaron Katersky. "The Manhattan DA's Investigation
into Trump and the Stormy Daniels Hush Payment, Explained." *ABC
News*, 15 Mar. 2023, abcnews.go.com/US/manhattan-das-investigation-
trump-stormy-daniels-hush-payment/story?id=97951106

222 *FBI Attorney Admits Altering Email Used in FISA Application During
Crossfire Hurricane. U.S. Department of Justice, District of Connecticut*, 19

Aug. 2020, justice.gov/usao-ct/pr/fbi-attorney-admits-altering-email-used-fisa-application-during-crossfire-hurricane.

[223] Cole, Devan, Hannah Rabinowitz, and Casey Gannon. *"The Justice Department Can Keep Trying to Reindict Letitia James, but Is It Worth the Risks?"* CNN, 12 Dec. 2025, https://www.cnn.com/2025/12/12/politics/justice-department-can-keep-trying-reindict-letitia-james-risks/index.html

ABOUT THE AUTHOR

Drew Thomas Allen is the host of *The Drew Allen Show*, where he delivers unapologetic analyses of politics, culture, and media. A publicist for high-profile government officials, military leaders, and public figures, Allen exposes how narratives are manufactured and weaponized by Washington and the media.

Allen lives in Napa Valley, California where he works, writes, and broadcasts.

www.ingramcontent.com/pod-product-compliance
Lightning Source LLC
Chambersburg PA
CBHW050907260726
48660CB00001B/80